Broken Things

BOOKS BY DR. DeHAAN . . .

The Tabernacle

Simon Peter

Signs of the Times

The Chemistry of the Blood

Broken Things

Adventures in Faith

The Jew and Palestine in Prophecy

Studies in 1 Corinthians

508 Answers to Bible Questions

The Second Coming of Jesus

Revelation

Daniel the Prophet

Jonah

Our Daily Bread

The Romance of Redemption

Hebrews

Galatians

Genesis and Evolution

Bread for Each Day

Pentecost and After

Law or Grace

Coming Events in Prophecy

The Days of Noah

Portraits of Christ in Genesis

Broken Things

M. R. DeHaan, M.D.

Revised and Condensed by Dennis J. DeHaan

ZONDERVAN PUBLISHING HOUSE
OF THE ZONDERVAN CORPORATION
GRAND RAPIDS, MICHIGAN 49506

BROKEN THINGS

Copyright 1948 by Zondervan Publishing House
Grand Rapids, Michigan

Assigned to the Radio Bible Class, 1966
This edition © 1977 by Radio Bible Class

First large print edition 1982
ISBN 0-310-23277-5

Printed in the United States of America

To the thousands of God's patient sufferers,
THE SAINTS
who patiently endure affliction and whose
testimonies of God's faithfulness have
often encouraged and helped me over
the hard places, to the glory of
God and the comfort of His
saints,
THIS VOLUME IS DEDICATED

CONTENTS

FOREWORD

The messages in this volume were first broadcast many years ago by Dr. M. R. DeHaan over the Mutual network and independent radio stations at home and abroad. Later they appeared, along with several other sermons, in a hardbound book entitled *Broken Things*. The thousands of letters from shut-ins, the aged, and the afflicted clearly indicated a widespread need for these messages of comfort.

This book differs in arrangement from the earlier edition. The first four chapters establish the basic principle set forth in the Word of God that brokenness is a prerequisite to usefulness and service. The next six chapters set forth some of the reasons for both physical and mental infirmities. The last chapter casts the entire subject of suffering against the background of eternity. The content of these messages remains essentially the same as when they were preached. Only a minimum of editing and revision has been done. All Scripture passages are from the King James text and are taken from the New Scofield Reference Edition of the Bible.

Those who remember Dr. DeHaan's deep, commanding voice will hear it again reechoing through the pages of this little volume as he expounds the Word to comfort and challenge the reader. And those who did not know him will quickly sense that the author, himself a medical doctor, had a heart of compassion for God's suffering and despairing children.

With the hope and prayer that these messages will be a blessing to thousands of God's patient sufferers, they are sent forth in this latest edition to the glory of God.

DENNIS J. DEHAAN
Associate Editor,
Our Daily Bread

CHAPTER 1

THE NEED FOR BROKENNESS

For thus saith the LORD to the men of Judah and Jerusalem,
Break up your fallow ground, and sow not among thorns
(Jeremiah 4:3).

"BREAK UP YOUR fallow ground." This was the message the
prophet Jeremiah was commissioned to bring to the people of
Israel. Dark days were settling upon the nation, and Israel,
trusting in her false security, was permitting the enemy to
destroy her because she was not willing to bestir herself and
turn to the Lord. The people of Israel had longed for ease and
comfort and had permitted their opportunities and blessings
to remain unworked and undeveloped; therefore the Lord
compares their nation to fallow ground. Fallow ground is that
which is permitted to lie idle and uncultivated. Instead of
producing grain and fruit, the land becomes covered with
weeds and thorns, and disaster lies ahead. So the prophet
calls to Israel, "Thus saith the LORD . . . Break up your fallow
ground, and sow not among thorns."

The spiritual applications of this expression are many and
profitable, but the one which comes to mind first of all is that
there can be no blessing without effort and no harvest without
plowing. Before a thing can be made, something must be

broken. Before the house is built, the tree must be broken down. Before the foundation can be laid, the rocks must be blasted from their quarry bed where they have long lain in peace and quiet. Before the ripe grain can cover the fields, the soil must be broken and beaten small. The cutting blade of the plow must turn over the sod, and the sharp teeth of the harrow must pulverize the soil. Before there can be life, there must be death. Before there can be joy, there must be weeping. The joy that floods the mother's heart at the sound of the first cry of her newborn babe was preceded by the tears of anguish of childbirth. Our Lord Jesus stated that principle in these words:

> Except a grain of wheat fall into the ground and die, it abideth alone; but if it die, it bringeth forth much fruit (John 12:24).

This is the law of life in the natural realm, and it is the law of life in the spiritual sphere also. There is no making without breaking. In the following messages we will study some of the many broken things found in the Bible and in everyday life. We are living in a broken world today. As never before, all that seemed permanent and enduring is being broken down; the history of the world is but the breaking of governments, systems, ideals, and programs. The history of every human life, too, is the history of breaking.

What memories come back out of the distant past as one traces again the tedious journey he began some years ago! Like misty shadows from the past they take form and materialize again, and he relives the days of sorrow over the broken things of life. The toys the children laughed over were broken and cast aside with the stain of childish tears upon them. How early in life the breaking processes begin! And then as he grew older, there were broken promises and broken hopes, shattered dreams, and unfulfilled ideals. Then after marriage he built his home and dreamed of peace and rest, but found that the increase of years increased also the weeping over broken things. All his expectations were shattered in a moment as the little darling in that home was rudely torn from his heart. Perhaps his wife, or his health, or his home, for which he had labored all his life in the anticipation that it would be the scene of quiet last days, were suddenly taken away. Yes, broken things are common in life. None can escape them.

To the child of God, however, every broken thing is but the assurance that God is making something. How needful it is for you who today are sorrowing over bitter losses and repining on beds of illness, you whose bodies are broken, to remember that He has said:

> And we know that all things work together for good to them that love God, to them who are the called according to his purpose (Romans 8:28).

If you are being broken by disappointment or bereavement, by loss or pain, by weakness or sickness, remember that although to us broken things are tragedies, to God they are opportunities to be used for His glory. We cast the *broken* things aside and call them "junk," but our God casts the *unbroken* things aside as useless.

BROKEN PITCHERS

To illustrate this truth and bring joy to many of you who today are being broken, we shall call attention to a great number of broken things mentioned in Scripture, showing that only the broken things are useful in God's wonderful dealings with us. In the seventh chapter of Judges we have the familiar story of Gideon, the sixth judge of the people of Israel after the death of Joshua. Israel was being vexed sorely by repeated attacks of her enemies the Midianites. When the people of God cried to the Lord for deliverance, God raised up a man by the name of Gideon to deliver them. The method of deliverance was unique, and after he had surrounded the camp of the enemy at night, Gideon gave the following instructions:

> When I blow with a trumpet, I and all that are with me, then blow ye the trumpets also on every side of the camp, and say, The sword of the LORD, and of Gideon.
>
> So Gideon, and the hundred men who were with him, came unto the outside of the camp. . . .
>
> And the three companies blew the trumpets, and broke the pitchers, and held the lamps in their left hands, and the trumpets in their right hands with which to blow; and they cried, The sword of the LORD, and of Gideon (Judges 7:18-20).

With pitchers in their hands, Gideon and his faithful 300 gained a dramatic and decisive victory in the routing of the Midianites. The record is familiar. Gideon was called of the Lord to go and fight the enemy. Some 32,000 had gathered themselves about him, but of all these volunteers, only 300 were fit. With these Gideon surrounded the camp of the enemy at night. In their hands they held trumpets and pitchers in which they had concealed blazing torches. At a command and signal from their captain the men were to break the earthen pitchers and thus let the light shine forth in the darkness. Then, blowing the trumpets, they gave the enemy the impression that instead of 300 men there were 300 companies of men who had surrounded them. The effect was stupendous. Fear gripped the enemy, and they fled in disorder throughout the night. The victory was complete.

We are interested in the part the broken pitchers played in the victory. The pitchers were earthen vessels, and hidden in them were flaming torches of light. We who have been saved are the earthen vessels to whom the Lord has entrusted the blessing of the Holy Spirit and the Word of Life. Within us dwells the Holy Spirit, the omnipotent Holy Spirit of God, the Spirit of Christ, by whom we can do all things. With Him nothing is impossible, for while it is true that without Him we can do nothing, it is equally true that we "can do all things through Christ, who strengtheneth" us. In the pitcher was the torch. The fire and the torch speak of the Spirit of power and victory.

Again and again the Holy Spirit, the only source of power and light in the Christian life, is referred to as fire. Fire is one of the many biblical symbols of the Holy Spirit. But this light has been placed in earthen vessels. Earthen vessels are the symbols of these human bodies of ours. At the wedding at Cana of Galilee, it was into empty vessels that the water was poured and made into wine, the symbol of joy and salvation, at the word of the Lord Jesus. It was in earthen vessels that the widow's small supply of oil was poured until all the vessels were filled. At best we are but earthen vessels to whom have been entrusted the words of life.

In the pitchers were torches. What a picture of the Christian as a result of regeneration! We have been endued with the Holy Ghost, and within every believer dwells the Holy Spirit with all the possibilities and potentialities of Omnipotence. At our disposal is placed the entire realm of Holy Ghost power. Yet the average believer goes through life without letting that power flow out. It seldom shines forth. Oftentimes there is darkness. So it was in Gideon's day. The torches were there, but there was no light and no victory until the pitchers were broken. Then the light shone forth and the enemy fled in consternation.

How we need to be broken. How often we bewail and bemoan the sad fact of broken lives, but find later that only broken things are used by the Lord and that only after we are broken are we our very best for God.

There are two possibilities in the Christian life. One is to be in the light, and the other is to walk in the light — to have light within and to let it shine out. The one possibility is life; the other is the life abundant. There is a carnal Christian, and there is a spiritual Christian. We may have, as we read in the fourth chapter of John, the water of life springing up within us; then again, we may have rivers of living water flowing forth out of us, as Jesus said in the seventh chapter of John. Light may be in the pitcher, but the pitcher must be broken if there is to be victory and power.

A BROKEN BODY

> This is my body, which is broken for you (1 Corinthians 11:24).

This quotation by Paul of the words of Jesus at the institution of the Lord's Supper voices a principle which, when properly understood, is of great comfort in times of trial and tribulation. Without the broken body of the Lord Jesus we could not be made whole. In God's wise counsel everything must be broken before it can be used fruitfully. Jesus expressed the same truth when He said,

> Except a grain of wheat fall into the ground and die, it abideth alone; but if it die, it bringeth forth much fruit (John 12:24).

What a world of memory there is contained in the words "broken things," which characterize the journey of life from the cradle to the grave. Even at birth we must be broken away from our mothers; and as we journey down life's pathway, until at last the "silver cord is loosed" and the "pitcher broken at the fountain," our course is strewn with broken things. From the earliest days of consciousness, man is in a world of broken things. The crying of the infant over a broken toy, the weeping of the child over the broken sled or kite, the sorrow of the young man over a broken trust are common in this world of broken things. There is the broken heart of the mother as the babe she has nursed at her bosom crushes her heart by his waywardness; there is the sorrow of the faithful wife who sits alone in the late hours of the night with broken heart and shattered confidence waiting for the one she once thought loved her. All along the way lie fragments of things that once were hopes and joys, things that were fashioned into dreams of happiness by the hand of fancy on the wheel of hope. That child who was the dream of all your love breaks your dreams. That business venture you envisioned fails. As the days go by, there are more and more of these broken things; and as the twilight of life comes and the old man totters to the broken sod, he looks back upon a world of broken things.

A Broken World

Broken homes, broken hearts, broken bodies, broken hopes, broken health, broken vows, broken lives — what sadness in those words! But this is merely the course of nature. Broken things suggest accidents and calamities. We associate them with disappointments and failure. But all these "tragedies" are known to God, and He can bring out of those broken fragments something far better, more beautiful, more enduring than that precious thing which was broken at our feet. With the Lord there are no calamities. God knows no disappointments. He knows all things from the beginning, and nothing which happens surprises Him. Knowing everything from the beginning, He has so planned that every broken piece in the lives of His own children will fit in somewhere in the complete portrait of His eternal counsel and will.

Are you being broken today upon a bed of illness or by a heart which grieves over the bitterness of a love spurned and abused? Here is comfort for you. God knows all about it, and He would not permit it if He did not see that in the end it will serve a purpose you do not now know.

I long ago learned the lesson — but need to remind myself of it constantly that God makes only what He breaks and breaks only what He wants to make. If you are being broken, God is working with you. He is making something — something which will someday astound you with its wisdom and beauty. Each time I have passed through the dark vale of disappointment and have cried in agony, "Oh, why, why must this be?" God has always led me out of the gloom into a greater light, out of the straits into a larger place. Someone has said, "The narrow straits always lead into the wide, wide ocean." The Lord deals with us in that way. The things we thought were the greatest trials and tragedies are found later to be God's way of bringing us something better. We think broken things are a loss, but God turns them to gain. In nature, broken things are cast aside; but in grace, God will never use a man until he is broken.

NATURE AND GRACE

Grace is always the reverse of nature. In the natural realm the first is first, but Jesus says that in the realm of grace the "first shall be last." Nature says that the youngest shall serve the eldest, but grace says, "The elder shall serve the younger." Nature says, "He that would be greatest among you, let him lord it over all." But grace says, "He that would be greatest among you, let him be your minister." If you are being broken by disappointment, by bereavement, by loss, by pain, by sickness, remember that while to us broken things are tragedies and worthless, they are the only things God can use.

The Bible is full of illustrations which support this truth. Again and again God uses broken things to gain the victory. Genesis speaks of a broken fellowship, but God uses it for the exhibition of His grace. Exodus tells of a broken law, but God uses it to prove to man his need of salvation and grace. Numbers depicts a broken covenant. In the Psalms we read about the outpouring of a broken and contrite heart. Samuel tells of a man with a broken back who sat at the king's table. Judges speaks of the broken pitchers in the hands of 300 men. In Matthew we read of broken loaves in the hands of Jesus. Mark tells of a broken roof which enabled a paralytic to approach Jesus for healing. In Luke we read of a broken alabaster box; and John tells of a broken home where Lazarus had died. We think of the broken net and the broken ship, the pieces of which helped to save Paul and his companions during a storm. We remember also the broken body of our Lord on the tree, and we hear Him saying to His disciples, "This is my body, which is broken for you." In each of these examples the breaking was for a purpose. In every instance a blessing resulted that so far outshone everything else that the pain of breaking was soon forgotten.

A BROKEN LAW

Of the many, many broken things mentioned in the Bible, we want to consider first the broken law of God. You will remember that after God had delivered His people out of the land of Egypt and had led them through the sea into the wilderness, they came to Mount Sinai. There God wanted to teach Israel the truth of grace. It may seem strange when I say that He gave them the law to teach them the need of grace, but it is true. There upon the mountain God gave by the hand of Moses two tables of stone, and on these tables of stone God wrote the law. There are some shallow-thinking Christians who imagine that the tables of stone were the law, but they were no different from thousands of other stones which abounded in that region. What was written on those stones constituted God's law. Before Moses could bring that law to the people to whom it was given, they had already broken it. Moses did not break the law when he cast the tables at the foot of the Mount. Israel had already broken it when they desired the golden calf and were dancing about it. Moses' breaking of the stones was a pictorial demonstration of the seriousness of Israel's sin.

ISRAEL MUST DIE

The broken law demands death. The law was never given to

save. The law was never meant to take a man to heaven. God knew before He gave the law that there would not be a son of Adam who would ever keep that law. Yea, we may go further and say that God never expected even one sinner to keep that law. It was given by God to reveal the need of grace.

That law was perfect and holy and just. It was the perfect expression of the perfect will of God, and imperfect man could not keep it because it was holy. Sinners could not attain to it. And because it was just, it must condemn everyone who broke it. "The soul that sinneth, it shall die" is the language of the law. "The wages of sin is death," says God's law. "Cursed is every one that continueth not in all things which are written in the book of the law to do them," says the law! God knew that Israel would break that law. God expected that they would. God knew the heart of man far too well to expect that he could keep His perfect law. He knew that in man, that is in his flesh, "dwelleth no good thing." That law must be broken to convince man that he needed grace. The breaking of the law by Israel was the proof and demonstration that "by the deeds of the law" there should "no flesh be justified in his sight." The broken law became the occasion for the revelation of the grace of God.

THE TABERNACLE

When Moses came down from the Mount, he carried, in addition to the tables of the law, the pattern of the tabernacle. The tabernacle is the exhibition of God's grace, just as the law is the expression of God's justice. The law knows no mercy. The law demands punishment for all who break it; and therefore if no more than the law had been given, man would be forever lost. But God now introduced the tabernacle — the great type of the Lord Jesus Christ and redemption by blood. Every part of that tabernacle spoke of Jesus Christ, but He was symbolized particularly by one article of furniture in the Holy of Holies. It was the ark of the covenant, the great picture of redemption through Jesus Christ. The ark, which rested in the Holy of Holies, was an oblong box made of wood and overlaid with gold. In the box, together with other articles, was the broken law — not the literal stones which Moses broke, but the second tables which contained the law that Israel had broken. This law called for judgment and the curse and death. It cried for vengeance. It was the ministration of death.

THE MERCY SEAT

But God made provision for Israel. Even though they had broken the law, they could be saved, for over this broken law in the ark was a mercy seat. Note the following carefully: Once a year the high priest took blood from the altar in the outer court (a type of the cross of Christ), carried it into the holiest place, and solemnly sprinkled that blood on the mercy seat over and above the broken law which demanded death and judgment and the curse. And then when God, the holy and the just One, came down in the Shekinah cloud of glory in the Holy of Holies, He saw the blood instead of beholding the broken law which demanded the eternal death of the sinner. The blood covered the law. The law which demanded blood ("without shedding of blood is no remission") had been satisfied by that blood. God would not curse His people who were under the blood, for He had said "When I see the blood, I will pass over you" (Exodus 12:13).

"WHEN I SEE THE BLOOD"

God looked upon the blood and was reconciled. Israel was safe. The law was broken by Israel, and what a tragedy it seemed. Yet it was God's way of revealing to His people their need of His grace and the power of the atoning blood. And God has not changed His method of dealing. He is still just and holy and must condemn the sinner and punish sin. No man can be saved by the law. The law stands to condemn you, but God has provided another Lamb of atonement whose blood was shed on the cross of Calvary and whose body was broken there to save those who had broken His law. There is then only one place of safety and shelter from the wrath of God, and that is "under the blood." He has said, "Without shedding of blood is no remission." Yes, the broken law calls for a broken Savior, and the broken Savior calls for a broken heart. Only through things broken can blessing come. Even Jesus could not be a Savior without being broken. God permitted man to break His holy law to convince him of his need for a broken Savior.

ARE YOU BROKEN?

Some of you are being broken today in body, in spirit, and in material things. Remember — until Jesus was broken He could not be your Savior. That is God's way of doing things. Some of the ingredients of the holy anointing oil in the tabernacle had to be crushed before they were used because, until they were crushed, their fragrance could not flow forth. For this reason we read:

> And thou shalt beat some of it very small, and put of it before the testimony in the tabernacle of the congregation (Exodus 30:36).

Until the incense was crushed, it could not give forth its fragrance. Until Christ was broken, He could not be our Savior. Except He, the grain of wheat, be broken and ground to flour, He could not be the Bread of Life to us. Oh, friend, do you realize that only the death of Christ can save you? Only as His body was broken, which means that His blood was allowed to flow out, could He atone for your sin. Without His blood there is no salvation. Are *you* under that blood? Then you have been redeemed from the curse of the law. But if you are not under the blood, you are still under the curse.

CHAPTER 2

A BROKEN ROOF AND A

BROKEN SHIP

IN THE SECOND chapter of Mark we read the interesting and instructive story of four men who brought a paralytic to the Lord Jesus Christ by breaking the roof of a house. Jesus had been teaching in a home in Capernaum. A great crowd soon assembled until they filled the house. People were crowded around the outside, making it impossible for anyone to get near the door to see and hear Jesus. But in Capernaum was a man who was afflicted with a dreadful disease because of a sinful life. He was, humanly speaking, hopeless. He could not walk. He had no means of getting to the Lord Jesus, but he did have four friends who were interested in him. The other folk had all flocked to hear the Lord Jesus for themselves and had forgotten about the poor man who had no way of enjoying the same blessing. I fear that in these days there are many similar situations. There are many people who are so busy learning theology and feeding upon the blessed truth of the Lord Jesus Christ that they forget their duty toward the poor sinners round about who have never gazed in faith upon His blessed face.

FOUR MEN AND A SINNER

Can you not see them coming down the dusty road? They had

made an improvised ambulance, probably similar to a stretcher, and on this the poor fellow lay. But as they came to the house, they found so many folk crowded around the Lord Jesus that there was no room to bring a poor sinner to Him. What a tragedy! There were so many people who wanted to hear His teaching that there was no room for a poor sinner to come to Christ! We are living in a day similar to that. Amid all the divisions and separations among believers, both in and out of the denominations, we are so busy defending the Book and discussing fine points of doctrine that we have forgotten the greatest desire and commission of the Lord Jesus. That this interpretation is not incorrect is clearly borne out by the fact that Jesus immediately stopped teaching the crowd and applied Himself to the more important business of saving and healing this poor paralytic.

Again the story emphasizes the need for our bringing men to Christ if they are ever going to come. The Lord has so ordered the plan of salvation that men and women are saved only as we bring them to Him. Man by nature is not sick. He is dead! He is impotent and as unable to find Christ without help as a dead man is unable to come forth from the grave. John 4 tells of the father who came to Jesus in his son's behalf. Because there was no man to put the paralytic into the pool, he lay helpless for thirty-eight years. Because the friends of Lazarus notified Jesus, showed Him where the tomb was, and took away the stone from the mouth of the sepulcher, Jesus raised the body of Lazarus. Because four men were more interested in this poor man than they were in hearing Jesus, this fellow was saved. Humanly speaking, he would have died in his sin and disease were it not for the interest these four men had in his condition.

God can make a bumper crop of wheat grow on the pavement of Fifth Avenue in New York City without help from man, but He has never done it, and He never will. God's way of raising a crop of wheat depends upon man. It is only as the farmer plows and drags and sows and cares for his acre that the Lord gives the increase — though He is omnipotent and needs no help from man. Likewise, in the spiritual realm, God could save every human being without the help of His children, without a tract or a dollar or a missionary. But God does not do things that way. It is God's plan that men will be saved only through the instrumentality of others. His commission is "Go ye, go ye, and preach the gospel." "Faith cometh by hearing, and hearing by the word of God." God has given us the commission and placed at our disposal the only two necessities for soul-winning: the Word and the Holy Spirit. If men are not saved, it will not be His fault, but ours, and ours alone. God has chosen to use no other way to make the gospel known than by telling from person to person the blessed truth of the Word.

A broken roof was the only means of getting this man to the Lord Jesus. These men were in earnest. The matter was not a side issue with them; they forgot everything else in their eagerness to help this man. They could not get through the door, and evidently a window was not available, either. What could they do? Necessity is the mother of invention, so these men made their way to the roof, and their friend was lifted. Then they began to break the roof. Can you imagine the effect on the crowd? Can you not hear a grumbler demand that someone make "those maniacs quit disturbing the meeting"? But not a word from the Lord. He must have been pleased. It is remarkable that no one succeeded in stopping them from breaking the roof. Perhaps the Lord intervened. Anyhow, the roof was open, and lo and behold a man on a bed was lowered into the crowd. The old, bald-headed hypocrites grumbled some more and made the fastest moves they ever made to keep from getting under the bed.

Notice the conduct of Jesus. Not a word of surprise. Not a rebuke for breaking up a Bible class to save a soul. Not a word because the decorum of the meeting had been disturbed. But Mark tells us,

> When Jesus saw their faith, he said unto the sick of the palsy, Son, thy sins are forgiven thee (Mark 2:5).

Two words need special consideration here: "Their faith." Not the sick man's faith, but *their faith*. I know that men are saved by their own personal faith in Jesus Christ and that you cannot be saved by *my* believing, yet it is true that men and women are being lost because of *our* lack of faith. It is equally true that people do find Jesus through the faith of others. It was through the faith of a Paul who dared to trust God that the gospel came to Europe, and you and I are saved because of Paul's faith. It is true that because David Livingstone had faith enough to trust God and blaze a gospel trail into the heart of Africa thousands were saved. Men are perishing because *we* have no faith. There are some who read this whom God wants on the foreign field, but you do not have enough faith to go.

There are some of you who have enough of this world's goods to support a half-dozen missionaries, but because you dare not trust God with what belongs to Him, thousands will slip into eternity without Christ. O God, make us dead in earnest! Set us on fire! Help us to break up our homes if need be to bring this paralyzed, dying world to Christ. Many of us have pleasant roofs over our heads. With much labor we have made a comfortable place for ourselves while the world is perishing for lack of Christ. Oh, for a zeal that will make us willing to "tear up the roof" and forget all false propriety and selfish endeavor to bring the message to those who never heard it!

Think of Christ. It was He who said, "This is my body, which is *broken for you*." He had a home in heaven, but He left it all and came and dwelt as a man, despised and rejected, a friend of sinners. He went all the way to Calvary to die that *you* might live.

Here is what is wrong with the church. We have lost our vision of the reality of the terribleness of the condition of lost man. Sin is real! Hell is real! The danger is real! Yet too often we are more concerned about the roof over our heads than the foundation under our feet. Parents, let me ask you, what is your greatest concern in life? Too often we view with apathy the evidences of unregeneration in our children. We seem so little concerned that our children, whom we love, are on the way to destruction and will spend eternity in hell, where they'll suffer the pangs of the wrath of God because we were more interested in their temporal needs than their spiritual needs. We rejoice over the material prosperity of our children but weep few tears over the fact that they are lost.

O God, help us to break the roof of materialism and worldly interest and open up the house to heaven until the answer comes down! We are not in earnest as we should be. Lord, break our hearts for Thee! Grant us visions of Thy compassion for the souls of men!

A BROKEN SHIP

Paul was a prisoner. He was on his way to Rome to appear before Caesar. A few weeks before, the ship's captain had set sail for Rome against the advice and warning of Paul; and now for two weeks they had been tossed about by the storm. Finally the ship crashed upon the rocks and the waves dashed it to pieces. In the scriptural record of the experience we read,

> And the rest, some on boards, and some on *broken pieces* of the ship. And so it came to pass that they all escaped safely to the land (Acts 27:44).

No doubt the ship was a very fine vessel. The fact that the sailors dared to set out at that season of the year suggests that it must have been a seaworthy vessel. But no ship of man's building can ever weather the storms of God. Here was a captain and his sailors who trusted their ship. A preacher warned them and said, "Do not go, for a storm is coming." But they did not believe Paul until the ship was dashed in pieces upon the rocks and they were all thrown overboard.

A parallel scene is being enacted every day in every country of the world. Man is trying to build himself a ship to cross the ocean of life and bring him safely to the harbor on the other side. This building is going on everywhere. The various religions of the world testify to man's desire and attempts to build for himself a ship which will carry him safely. Good works, morality, charity, philanthropy, culture, refinement, honesty, asceticism, fraternalism, politics, and all the rest of the leaky boats of human construction are being tried. Millions and millions of people today are trying to find a Utopia on these ships. But every ship constructed by man *must* fail. There is a storm coming, and every one of these boats will go down. We read in this chapter in Acts that when a south wind blew, the boatmen thought all was well and set out. But soon they ran into the storm. While the sun shines, these ships may seem trustworthy; but when the storm comes, all have been found to fail.

Sinner, what is your hope of heaven? Are you trusting in a ship of your own building? It will smash to pieces on the rocks by-and-by. Your own life, yea, and works cannot avail. Your righteousness is as filthy rags in God's sight.

> Not by works of righteousness which we have done, but according to his mercy he saved us (Titus 3:5).

> But to him that worketh not, but believeth on him that justifieth the ungodly, his faith is counted for righteousness (Romans 4:5).

Sinner, have you believed? You must be broken. All your efforts will never save you. You must abandon your own ship no matter how much it may cost you or how much you cherish it. It was on broken pieces of the ship that Paul and his companions came to land. When you abandon the old ship of your own merits and cast yourself before God, He will save you. They were not saved by their ship but were saved by the breaking of their ship. If the ship had not been broken, there would have been no pieces; and if there had been no pieces, there would have been no hope.

> Verily, verily, I say unto you, He that heareth my word, and believeth on him that sent me, hath everlasting life, and shall not come into judgment, but is passed from death unto life (John 5:24).

CHAPTER 3

BROKEN LOAVES AND A

BROKEN BODY

IN THE FIFTEENTH chapter of Matthew we have the story of the feeding of the 4,000. The entire setting is suggestive. For three days the crowds had been following the Lord Jesus in the wilderness and listening to the gracious words which fell from His blessed lips. Eventually, however, their food supply was gone. A hungry crowd does not make the best kind of audience for a preacher. A man is more likely to be thinking of his stomach's needs at such a time than of his heart's needs; so the Lord prepared to meet that situation. Of course, He could have made the manna rain again from heaven, or He could have made loaves of bread grow on the bushes. But God does not work that way. He said to the disciples, "You give them to eat." When they demurred at the seeming impossibility, He inquired what they had to eat and found that there were still seven loaves of bread and a few fishes for the disciples and their Lord — enough for their immediate needs, but certainly nothing more. They needed all they had. Jesus said, "Let me have them." When He had given thanks, He broke the loaves and the fishes and handed them back to the disciples. They in turn passed them to the multitude, and they all did eat and were filled. When they gathered up the fragments, they had seven baskets full. The bread had increased a hundredfold or more.

The miracle is also a parable. We too are in a wilderness. It is a dry and thirsty land. This world can never satisfy the human heart. It is not big enough. The heart of man was created for infinity. It was made to be the dwelling place of the infinite God. Only God can fill and satisfy the human heart, and because the human heart was made to embrace Him, nothing less can ever satisfy it. Someone has said that a round world can never fill a triangular heart. There will always be corners which must remain empty. Only the Triune God can fill and satisfy the heart of man. What a hungry world we are living in today! The lust for power, the millions spent in pursuit of pleasure — these are vain attempts to answer the universal cry of the human heart for something that is missing. To this poor, starving, dying world, Jesus says, "I have compassion on them. I will not send them away empty. You give them to eat."

We say, as did the disciples, "Where will we get enough to feed all these?" But Jesus replies, "You have enough. You have enough if you will only share it." "Why, we have only seven little loaves! We have so little. What can we do?" we say in despair.

Then the Lord Jesus gives us the most sublime truth in the Word: "If you will give Me your little, I will break it up for you and let you give it to others. Then I'll return it to you increased a hundredfold."

Note well the order of events: we give ourselves and what we have to Him; He takes the little and increases it; then we take it to others and are enriched ourselves beyond all imagination. It is not what we have but what we surrender to Him that counts. We can never give this poor old starving world a thing until we have first given ourselves to God.

Think of the world today. There are hundreds of millions of men and women, Jews and Gentiles, who have not yet heard the message of the blessed Christ. Faint and hungering in the wilderness of this world, they are turning to religion and pleasure and sin and debauchery to quiet that yearning for something which will satisfy. Hear their cry! The world has been full of quacks who have offered to give the suffering souls nostrums and patent medicines to relieve their ills. The theater, the dance, the liquor bottle, the bright lights are offered — but they only make the hunger deeper, the throat more parched, and the heart more empty. Others attempt to satisfy the heart with the social gospel, good works, philanthropy, education, philosophy, and travel; yet the cry goes up, "Give us to eat!" And we are the only ones who have anything permanent to give these starving souls. When Christians are willing to place in the hands of the Lord the little they have, He will do great and marvelous things.

BROKEN LOAVES

They were the disciples' loaves. They were theirs until Jesus needed them. Will you give your loaves to Him? Young man, you have a life. It is not your life only; Jesus is asking for it. Will you let Him have it and break it up and feed it to a dying multitude? You have hoped to give your life to a prosperous career in business or in the professions. You have an education. You are ready to make good. The world offers you success and money, popularity and pleasure. But Jesus asks for your life. He wants to use it in the ministry, or on the foreign field, or somewhere else. But such service and surrender means the breaking up of ideals, plans, and dreams. Jesus says of your life, "Let Me have it." "What will I have for myself?" you ask. Jesus gives the answer: "If you will be ready to give your all for those who are dying, I will take care of you. Give your bread to those whom I died to save, and I will take care of you."

Hallelujah! I have found it so. I have eaten from the seven baskets which were left over after I placed my all on the altar for Christ and left a profitable medical practice for the toughest job on earth — the task of preaching the gospel.

Broken loaves! The loaves of your life, your talents, your education, your ideals! Say, "Here they are, Lord Jesus! Here is my money." God has given some of you several golden loaves. He has blessed you with wealth and material things. You thanked God as you nibbled their sweetness. You praised Him as you buttered that bread while millions of others were starving for the Bread of Life. Oh, you may have thanked God for giving you the loaves, but have you heard His call to give them to others?

> Give, and it shall be given unto you; good measure, pressed down, and shaken together, and running over, shall men give into your bosom. For with the same measure that ye measure it shall be measured to you again (Luke 6:38).

Seven loaves — seven baskets! How I would that God would convert a dozen millionaires and give them the grace to take the seven loaves and let them be broken for this dying world.

This old world is dying without Christ, and we have the gospel. God is asking only that we entrust to His hand the few loaves we have and let them be broken. We need to be broken to a vision of the need of lost souls. We confess that we believe a man is lost without Christ and goes to an eternal hell. We talk about it, write about it — and then do so tragically little about it.

I am pleading for broken loaves, for broken hearts, for broken men — men broken from their selfishness, broken from their indifference, broken from their covetousness, broken from their lethargy, and awakened to the profitableness and glory of being out and out for God. Let Him have whatever you have. Say with the hymnwriter,

O Cross that liftest up my head,
  I dare not ask to fly from Thee;
I lay in dust life's glory dead,
And from the ground there blossoms red
  Life that shall endless be.

A Broken Body

"This is my body . . . broken for you." Thus did the Lord Jesus speak of His death when He took the bread and broke it before His disciples. He never asks us to do something which He has not done. If what we have been speaking of in these pages seems hard — too hard — one look at Calvary should stop all complaining. There the Son of God hung on the cross as the sin-bearer of the world. Broken things are the result of sin. If sin had never entered, our world would not be broken as it is. There would have been no broken promises, no broken laws, no broken trusts, no broken hearts and homes and hopes, no broken bodies and spirits and dreams, no bleeding wounds. But the broken things may be overruled and made to glorify the wisdom of God. He sent His Son to be broken that all these might be healed. Nineteen hundred years ago He came and began a work of redemption which, although it was potentially finished when He died on Calvary, awaits the consummation when He shall put all things under His feet and make all things new.

His body was broken literally also — broken when they scourged Him and the skin burst open and the raw flesh stood out — broken when they crowned Him with thorns and the cruel barbs sank into His blessed brow — broken when they drove the cruel nails through His blessed hands and feet and impaled Him on a tree — broken when they pierced His side and the water and the blood came forth to testify to the reality of His suffering as well as His death — broken for us. I can see Him standing there with the bread in His hands as He said to those at the table, "This is my body which is broken for you."

Now He asks only that we be broken for Him; that we break these earthen pitchers and let His light shine. The apostle voices this truth:

> I beseech you therefore, brethren, by the mercies of God, that ye present your bodies a living sacrifice, holy, acceptable unto God (Romans 12:1).

Our Savior asks that we give to Him our few loaves and fishes so that He may increase them for us and give them back to us to give to others. We cannot escape His command:

> Go ye into all the world, and preach the gospel to every creature (Mark 16:15).

He asks that we break up the roofs that we have carefully made for our own pleasure and turn things upside down in our zeal to bring men to Christ.

He asks that we take the alabaster box, break it, and pour it over His head in some service for Him.

He asks that we learn the lesson of the broken net and trust Him fully.

He asks that you, sinner, abandon the ship of your own righteousness and throw yourself on the cross where Jesus was broken for you. If Paul's fellow voyagers had stayed on the ship, they would all have been lost. Their salvation lay in their leaving the ship.

We cannot be His until we are broken of self, and we cannot be instruments fit for God's use until our hearts have been broken by penitence and our lives rent by suffering. Claim the comfort of His promise, the promise which cannot be broken:

> In the world ye shall have tribulation: but be of good cheer; I have overcome the world (John 16:33).

> Many are the afflictions of the righteous; but the Lord delivereth him out of them all (Psalm 34:19).

CHAPTER 4

A BROKEN VASE

As WE STUDY the broken things of the Bible, each becomes more precious and beautiful. The fourteenth chapter of Mark tells of a broken alabaster box of ointment poured out upon the blessed head of our Lord Jesus. A great deal of conjecture has attended these words, and no definite answer can be given as to the exact identity of the woman mentioned in the passage. Some say that she was Mary of Bethany, the same woman who anointed the Lord Jesus as told in the twelfth chapter of John. Others point out that this can hardly be so because the account in John tells us that Jesus was entertained in the home of Lazarus, whereas Mark's record speaks of Jesus in the house of Simon the leper. Others say that this Mary was the sinful woman who had been so marvelously saved from a life of sin by the Lord Jesus. We shall not dogmatize. Enough that the Holy Spirit does not give her name in this passage before us. If we suppose that she was a sinful woman who had been forgiven by the Lord, we shall not fall short of the mark.

There is an interpretation which tells us that this precious vase of ointment was a cosmetic used by the women in Jesus' day, especially by those women who sought to beautify themselves for baser purposes. To suppose that this is true only makes the narrative more instructive. Here is a woman who had been living a life of sin. She resorted to the age-old and yet modern scheme of adorning and perfuming herself to cover her corruption so that she might more easily entrap her victims. But then a man had crossed her path. His name was Jesus. Before He left her, she had been saved and cleansed by His power, and her bitter life of sin and shame had been changed into a song of eternal gladness. Virtue replaced vice; glory replaced shame. This had happened some time before. Now she knew the Lord would soon be gone, and her one desire was that she might pour upon His head the very things which in days past she had used for her sinful career. So she broke her precious ointment and poured it upon the head of her Redeemer. She gave to Him the devotion which she had once given to her life of sin.

What a lesson for us! Many of us remember how we served the world in days gone by. We held nothing back. We served the devil with all our might. No hours were too late, no expense too great, no sacrifice too costly. We were willing to spend and be spent for the sinful fleeting pleasures of the world. Many a costly vase of ointment was lavished upon ourselves or our sinful friends. But when Jesus came into our lives, He became ours. We still possess those same powers and abilities which we gave to the devil, but our time and our education and our talents can no longer be used for the world. Have we taken the alabaster box and poured it over His head with the same lavish abandon and liberality that we sacrificed to the world? Consider the use of your time. Do you remember that before your conversion you could sit until one o'clock in the morning at the card table, or spend hours at the poolroom or the bowling alley? But now if the church service lasts a bit too long you complain and stay at home to listen to the radio so that you can turn it off at will. How we shouted at games and parties, but how seldom do we sound a note of praise to God!

Do you remember the money you spent for pleasure and worldly amusements? Not nickels and dimes, but bills — fives and twenties and even more in one evening. Now, though that alabaster box is as full of money as before, you merely take the lid off and let the Lord have a smell of it, while you carefully keep the rest for yourself. While missions are pleading and begging, you are carefully sealing the alabaster box. How I wish that I could make all born-again believers as liberal for the cause of the Lord as they were for the devil before they were saved!

The box must be broken. Nothing less will do. Now there are several things this woman could have done, and I suppose everyone in the house would have thought her action splendid. She could have taken off the cover of the box and poured a teaspoonful of the ointment on His head, or she could have emptied all the ointment upon His head and kept the bottle so that she could fill it again and anoint herself. But she did not. She broke the vase. She destroyed every possibility that anyone else would be anointed with the contents of that bottle. Do you see the meaning of the act? It was not something to be repeated. It was an act of consecration which was final as far as the woman's yielding herself to Him was concerned. The box could be broken only once, and it could never be repaired.

How many there are whose lives resemble the broken alabaster box! It is true of most men of God who have really been used of the Lord that somewhere in their lives there was a crisis, a test in which they were broken. And they could date from that day a new inflow of power and outflow of service. I am convinced that the great need of Christians today is a breaking of the vase once and for all. I am not thinking of a second blessing nor a second definite work of grace. Grace is something God does. I am speaking of something you do when you yield yourself and lie broken at His feet.

The woman broke the vase. Here was a woman who refused to be hampered by tradition. To my knowledge, such a thing had never been done. It was without precedent, but her very greatness lay in the fact that she dared to be different. We have been carrying on our church work in the same traditional, musty way for so long that anyone who dares to depart from the moss-covered methods of the past is considered a novice and an upstart fanatic. But history reveals that progress comes when someone is willing to be different. Whitefield, when he went outdoors to preach because no building was big enough, was ridiculed for his "foolishness." How could he expect a blessing outdoors? Unheard of! Unreasonable! The church — that was considered the place of blessing. But Whitefield went, and God blessed, and one of the mightiest revivals swept the world. Dare to be different! Dare to be a fool for Christ's sake!

The woman broke the vase. We have already anticipated that it was a final act. But it had even further significance. The woman wanted to let it be known that this act was for Him exclusively without thought of self or anyone else. Martha was serving, but not exclusively for Him. It was in His honor, but it was for others, too. Simon entertained our Lord, but others were included. But what this woman did was for Christ alone.

What is much of our service these days? Is it for Him or for something or someone else? Imagine if you can the Lord Jesus Himself standing before you as He hung on Calvary. His hands are outstretched and pierced with nails. See what He did for you. What have you done for Him that can begin to compare with what He did for you? "Oh," you may say, "I have worshiped Him in God's house.'' Yes, but that was for *your* profit, too. ''Well, but I pray.'' Yes, for things *you* need. ''I read His Word.'' Yes, and that is profitable to *you*. Do you ever sing just to please *Him?* Do you teach Sunday school because you seek to do something for *Him?* Is it a passion for others or love for *Him* that prompts your service? Do you serve as an officer because you are interested in the church, or because you want to help the pastor? Or do you do it for *Him?*

I sometimes wonder whether I have ever done anything just for Him. When I look at Him, everything I have done seems so small, so negative. If I were to give up my work here and go to Africa and suffer and work and sweat among the blacks there, that would be nothing in comparison with what He has done for me. I do not expect all of you to feel as I do regarding my debt to my Savior, for perhaps you do not owe Him as much as I do. Perhaps you have not sinned as I have, and you have not had so much forgiven. But I know that if every atom in this body were a man, and every one of these millions of men could suffer untold agonies, I could never repay Him for what He has done for me.

CHAPTER 5

WHY WE SUFFER

THE GREATEST sermons I have ever heard were not preached from pulpits but from sickbeds. The greatest, deepest truths of God's Word have often been revealed not by those who preached as a result of their seminary preparation and education, but by those humble souls who have gone through the seminary of affliction and have learned experientially the deep things of the ways of God.

The most cheerful people I have met, with few exceptions, have been those who had the least sunshine and the most pain and suffering in their lives. The most grateful people I have met were not those who had traveled a pathway of roses all their lives through, but those who were confined, because of circumstances, to their homes, often to their beds, and had learned to depend upon God as only such Christians know how to do. The "gripers" are usually, I have observed, those who enjoy excellent health. The complainers are those who have the least to complain about, and those dear saints of God who have refreshed my heart again and again as they preached from sickbed-pulpits have been the men and women who have been the most cheerful and the most grateful for the blessings of almighty God.

The Bible tells us distinctly that there is a special reward and a special crown which the Lord has prepared and laid up for those who suffer patiently. This principle is suggested by the incident recorded in 1 Samuel 30:24. David with 400 strong, healthy men had gone out to seek the enemy. Two hundred, however, had remained behind because they were weary and faint, probably because of some physical infirmity. These David had left behind to care for the stuff of those who went into the heat of the battle. After the victory had been won, the 400 who had been in the active participation of David's army refused to share with those who had remained behind and said, ''We'll give them just a little bit, but we're going to take the spoils.'' At this point David stated the eternal principle in the words of 1 Samuel 30:24:

> As his part is who goeth down to the battle, so shall his part be who tarrieth by the baggage; they shall divide alike.

Those of you who remain by the stuff are not overlooked or forgotten of God: there is a very definite and special reward laid up for God's patient sufferers. If you are upon a bed of illness, if you are being troubled by pain and discouragement, remember that this is for a definite reason. We are going to discuss in this and the following chapters some of the scriptural explanations concerning the suffering of Christians.

Suffering Silences Satan

The first reason is this: God uses the experience of His children to silence the enemy of the Word of God and the Lord Jesus Christ. Probably the best example of this is the story of the patriarch Job. Remember that Job was a wealthy man, but he was also a spiritual and godly man. When the Lord called Satan's attention to the fact that Job was a godly man who feared the Lord perfectly with all his heart, the devil accused Job of doing it only for the gain and profit which came to him materially as a result of his fearing the Lord. You will recall that God gave Satan the privilege, the right, to lay his hand upon Job and to take away his possessions and his family. The result was that Satan was silenced, for Job, instead of murmuring and complaining and turning in bitterness against almighty God, praised the Lord and was able to say, "The Lord gave, and the Lord has taken away; blessed be the name of the Lord."

Is it not wonderful to think that God is willing to use us to silence the adversary, the devil, by the testing and the trials and the tribulations which come upon us? Many times I have stood at the bedsides of God's patient sufferers and have seen the enemy silenced — he who would say that we serve God only in sunshine. I can take you to the bedside of many who have been racked with pain for years, and I can show you smiles never seen on other faces. Those smiles which indicate gratitude and praise to God belong only to those who have been trained in the school of affliction. If you are one of God's "Satan-silencers," praise Him for it.

Suffering Enables Us to Glorify God

In the eleventh chapter of John's Gospel we find another reason the Lord permits calamity, trouble, pain, suffering, and sorrow to come upon His people. The eleventh chapter of John records the death of Lazarus, a very dear and precious friend of the Lord Jesus Christ. The Savior knew that Lazarus was sick. He could have healed him at a distance, but He deliberately permitted Lazarus to die in order that He might reveal some blessed truth which could not in any other way be taught to Lazarus and his two sisters. Therefore the Lord Jesus Christ, in the course of His conversation with His disciples, says, "This sickness is not unto death, but for the glory of God, that the Son of God might be glorified by it" (v. 4). The next verse tells us:

Now Jesus loved Martha, and her sister, and Lazarus (John 11:5).

Yet our Lord permitted Lazarus to die in order that He might be glorified by the death of one of His friends and that the joy of resurrection, which can never come except to those who have lost loved ones, might be the experience of these friends of the Lord Jesus Christ.

SUFFERING MAKES US MORE LIKE CHRIST

The third reason God permits His children to suffer is this: He can accomplish in this way the ultimate purpose for which He Himself has called and chosen us. The purpose of God in choosing and saving a man or a woman is to make that person more like the Lord Jesus Christ Himself. The Lord is not interested merely in saving you, keeping you out of hell, and taking you to heaven when you die. His purpose is much wider and deeper than providing salvation merely as a means of escaping punishment and entering into bliss at the end of life. We read in Romans 8:29:

> For whom he did foreknow, he also did predestinate to be conformed to the image of his Son, that he might be the firstborn among many brethren.

This is a precious truth from the Word of God. Those whom He foreknew were all in God's plan from eternity. He predestinated you not primarily to be saved from hell or to go to heaven when you die, but to be conformed to the image of His Son.

Now, if it is the purpose of the Lord ultimately to make us like the Lord Jesus Christ, that means there must be suffering, pain, and sorrow in our lives. No believer will ever be like Christ without these afflictions, similar to those which Christ experienced so deeply. We read, concerning the Lord Jesus Christ, in the Epistle to the Hebrews:

> For it became him, for whom are all things . . . in bringing many sons unto glory, to make the captain of their salvation perfect through sufferings (Hebrews 2:10).

And in the closing verse of that same chapter we read:

> For in that he himself hath suffered being tempted, he is able to help them that are tempted (Hebrews 2:18).

To be made like the Lord Jesus Christ implies that we follow Him in all things. This means not only the mount of the Transfiguration, but also the mount of Calvary, and the Garden of Gethsemane; it means darkness and suffering. That is why Paul could say in Philippians 3:10:

> That I may know him, and the power of his resurrection, and the fellowship of his sufferings, being made conformable unto his death.

O to be like the Lord Jesus Christ! We often sing:

> Earthly pleasures vainly call me,
> I would be like Jesus.
> Nothing worldly shall enthrall me,
> I would be like Jesus.
>
> Be like Jesus, this my song,
> In the home and in the throng,
> Be like Jesus all day long,
> I would be like Jesus.

And if we would be like Him, certainly then we must be willing to follow Him wherever He leads.

Suffering Makes Us Appreciative

Another reason for God's testing and trials is this: they make us more appreciative of the blessings which God bestows upon us. True, it is often more difficult to praise God when darkness besets us than when the sun is shining brightly, and yet it is also true that often we do not appreciate our blessings until they take flight. For example, how many of you shut-ins have never appreciated the ministry of gospel radio

47

broadcasts until you were laid aside in your home? Probably many of you had listened but were never moved to write a word of encouragement or appreciation to those who week after week sent these messages to you with their fervent prayers that God would bless the messages to your heart. Oh, yes, you were thankful for the radio ministry, and yet there was no deep sense of appreciation; and then you were laid aside upon a bed of illness, possibly because of an accident or some other reason. You were not able to fellowship with God's saints and go about like others, and you were made dependent upon the radio for your fellowship and worship. Then you began to appreciate the efforts and the sacrifice made by others in behalf of those who were not blessed as you were during the days of your health. Among these innumerable blessings that come to us when God sets us aside in His providence and in the wonderful provision which He has made according to Romans 8:28 — namely, "that all things work together for good to them that love God, to them who are the called according to his purpose" — we have this also, that suffering gives us a sense of appreciation which we can obtain in no other way.

Suffering Teaches Us to Depend Upon God

Another reason, and I think a very common reason, the Lord brings upon us the suffering and the pain which so often try us is that we may learn to depend upon the Lord and not rely upon our own strength.

> In returning and rest shall ye be saved; in quietness and in confidence shall be your strength (Isaiah 30:15).

The children of Israel had found themselves in difficulties and in straits, and instead of turning to the Lord, they had turned to an alliance with the nations around them, particularly the Egyptians. The Lord told them that their strength was not in the nations or in their army. But He said to them,

"In quietness and in confidence shall be your strength." How many of you during your days of health felt that you were indispensable in your work or your home or your business? You were convinced that if anything happened to you, everything would go wrong. You *had* to be there. You couldn't take time off from anything to be quiet. You rushed and fretted and hurried around and then the Lord, probably to rebuke you, laid you aside. Your business, your family, loved ones, and your work had to get along without you, and you found out to your surprise that they got along as well without you as with you. Yes, you found that when that day came, God was able to guide and direct and see you through experiences which you thought you could never endure.

I must confess that I had to learn that difficult but great lesson. Such education is hard on our pride. It makes us humble. It takes something out of us, and yet it teaches us that the Lord can get along without us and that we must learn to depend upon Him. We read in Exodus 14:13 that when the Israelites stood before the sea with the Egyptians behind them and deserts and mountains on each side, the Lord said, "Stand still, and see the salvation of the Lord."

Oh, the precious lesson He teaches us when we learn that God can undertake for us and do things far beyond our comprehension! The Bible says,

> Not by might, nor by power, but by my Spirit, saith the LORD of hosts (Zechariah 4:6).

Are you one of God's shut-ins? Did you have to learn some of these difficult lessons? Ah, then your life has been enriched, and I know that even now you can praise God for His wonderful dealings.

CHAPTER 6

WHY WE SUFFER

(continued)

> But he knoweth the way that I take; when he hath tested me, I shall come forth as gold (Job 23:10).

IT IS SAID that a bar of steel worth $5 when made into ordinary horseshoes will be worth only $10. If this same $5 bar is manufactured into needles, the value rises to $350, but if it is made into delicate springs for expensive watches, it will be worth $250,000. This original bar of steel is made more valuable by being cut to its proper size, passed through the heat again and again, hammered and manipulated, beaten and pounded, finished and polished, until it is finally ready for its delicate task.

This truly is a parable which sets forth a vital truth concerning the child of God. Let us realize that God expends His effort only on that which gives promise of having value. The farmer does not spend time tilling the sandhill that has no value for crops; he puts most of his work and time into the heavy field which has the greatest promise of an abundant harvest. When God leaves us utterly alone and does not visit us with difficulties and testings and trials, we may be sure that our lives are barren. Someone has said, ''Sunshine all the time only makes a desert." We need the clouds, the dark days, the storms, and the rain just as much as we need the sunshine. And God who is molding our lives, seeking to make us like the Lord Jesus Christ, is the One who knows what is best for us. In the verse that we quoted at the beginning of this chapter, we hear Job saying,

> But he knoweth the way that I take; when he hath tested me, I shall come forth as gold (Job 23:10).

Notice that Job does not say, "I know the way that He takes," but rather, "He knoweth the way that *I* take." We would like to know what God is doing. We would like to pull aside the veil and see the end from the beginning. We would like to know the way that He is taking, but if we did, and if we could see, we would not need faith to believe and to accept God's way. So Job, in the midst of all his deep afflictions, found comfort, not in the fact that he knew the reason and the answer for all of God's dealing with him, but in the truth that God knew what He was doing. "He knoweth the way that I take," he said confidently, and then his faith leaped over every barrier; and as he looked into the distant future, he cried, "When he hath tried me, I shall come forth as gold."

Probably we experience one of the most trying means by which God accomplishes His purpose in our lives when we are forced to sit still. When our hearts yearn to do something for Him, when we would like to be active and out in the world witnessing for Christ, when we long to do something important, probably even spectacular, then the Lord places us in a position of inactivity and causes us to learn the lesson of quietness and stillness. That, I believe, is one of the greatest tests of a Christian's faith. Yet, as we have pointed out in our previous chapter, those who remain behind with the stuff are as important as those who are found in the front lines of the battle. David said, "As his part is who goeth down to the battle, so shall his part be that tarrieth by the baggage."

In our previous chapter we indicated a few results of God's trial and testing in the life of a Christian. In this chapter we shall consider a few more of the almost innumerable lessons which only trouble and trial and persecution can teach us. The Word tells us,

> For we are saved by hope. But hope that is seen is not hope; for what a man seeth, why doth he yet hope for?
> But if we hope for that which we see not, then do we with patience wait for it (Romans 8:24,25).

God wants to strengthen our faith. Only exercise can give strength. We know how true this is in the physical realm. We must use our bodies and our muscles as well as our minds if they are to grow. The same is true of our faith. The faith which is not exercised is a faith which will not grow; a faith which is not tried will never be strong. Faith is believing what we cannot see and understand. According to Scripture, "faith is the substance of things hoped for, the evidence of things not seen." The very fact that you cannot understand why God deals with you in the way He does is for the purpose of making you exercise your faith. If we could understand all of God's dealings, we would not need faith. I need no faith to see a tree when my eyes are open or to hear the birds when my hearing is good, but to believe the things which we cannot see and cannot understand and cannot fathom — that is faith. We exercise faith when we accept the promise of almighty God. If you are laid aside and you have been asking the question, "Why must I suffer? Why cannot I be like others?" then remember that God says, "All things work together for good to them that love God, to them who are the called according to his purpose." That is God's promise. You may not understand why, but you receive and accept His Word, and you believe that what God sends to you is the best for you. You may claim this assurance with the hymnwriter:

I do not know why oft 'round me,
My hopes all shattered seem to be;
God's perfect plan I cannot see,
But someday I'll understand.

Someday He'll make it plain to me,
Someday when I His face shall see;
Someday from tears I shall be free,
For someday I shall understand.

Another purpose in God's dealings with us is to purify our lives and to make us more like the Lord Jesus Christ.

Beloved, think it not strange concerning the fiery trial which is to test you, as though some strange thing happened unto you,
But rejoice, inasmuch as ye are partakers of Christ's sufferings, that, when his glory shall be revealed, ye may be glad also with exceeding joy (1 Peter 4:12,13).

This tells us that we are to rejoice in the hope and the confidence that God's purpose is being accomplished in our lives.

SUFFERING TEACHES US PATIENCE

We have already touched upon the necessity of God's dealing with us in order that we may learn to be patient.

And hope maketh not ashamed, because the love of God is shed abroad in our hearts by the Holy Spirit who is given unto us (Romans 5:5).

That verse follows upon another verse:

But we glory in tribulations also (Romans 5:3).

I want you to notice that Paul was able to say, because he had advanced far in Christian experience, that we glory in tribulations also. It is not always easy to do this, and yet Paul could say it. Now notice why Paul was able to glory in tribulation:

. . . knowing that tribulation worketh patience; And patience, experience; and experience, hope; And hope maketh not ashamed . . . (Romans 5:3-5).

Patience can be learned only by enduring. Unless our patience, like our faith, is tried, we will never learn to be patient. Therefore, among the many, many blessed lessons and results of our tribulations and troubles and trials is this: We learn to be patient.

SUFFERING MAKES US SYMPATHETIC

> Blessed be God, even the Father of our Lord Jesus Christ, the Father of mercies, and the God of all comfort,
> Who comforteth us in all our tribulation, that we may be able to comfort them who are in any trouble, by the comfort with which we ourselves are comforted of God.
> For as the sufferings of Christ abound in us, so our consolation also aboundeth by Christ.
> And whether we be afflicted, it is for your consolation and salvation, which is effectual in the enduring of the same sufferings which we also suffer; or whether we be comforted, it is for your consolation and salvation (2 Corinthians 1:3-6).

Anyone who has felt the chastening hand of the Lord as He sought to mold and shape his life knows the truth of the statement that one can never be sympathetic toward others until he has needed sympathy himself. The world knows little about true Christian sympathy, about entering into the sufferings of others, and it is a fact that until we have suffered ourselves, we are, as Job says, "miserable comforters." The people who can bring the greatest comfort and peace into our hearts are those who can talk from personal experience. That is true not only of physical suffering, but of our spiritual life also. Those of us who seek to serve the Lord Jesus Christ can soon tell when we meet other Christians whether they have had a vital experience with the Savior. With such Christians we are able to fellowship. We talk the same language. The minutes and the hours fly by, and we feel refreshed and comforted as we exchange our experiences concerning the Lord Jesus Christ.

On the other hand, when we seek to carry on a conversation or fellowship with those who have not experienced the sweetness of a personal relationship to Christ through faith, how tedious the hours and the moments are, and how weary we become from that sort of false fellowship! The same is true of physical illness. Those who have been used of God to comfort us, to speak intelligently and understandingly in a way that brings comfort and peace and relaxation, are those who themselves have passed through the valley of testing and know whereof they speak.

I say this kindly, and yet it is true. During the illnesses and the days and the months that I have been permitted to be laid aside from the active ministry, there were a great many of my friends who came to visit. All of them, I believe, were sincere and earnest and well-meaning. They came with the intention of lifting the load and brightening the way and extending their sympathy. Yet as I look back upon those experiences, I can divide all of these friends into just two classes: those who helped me and those who hindered me. May I again repeat that I am saying this without harsh criticism, but as an experience of truth. There were first of all those who did their very best, but they didn't know what I had endured; they didn't know what I had experienced. They knew nothing of my pain and suffering and heartache and temptations. And so they sought to say something that might comfort me; and yet after they were gone, I had to say with Job of old, "Miserable comforters are they all."

But, ah, how sweet, how precious, how helpful was the ministry of those who came and, though they did not talk as much, by the very press of their hand and by relating their own experiences showed me immediately that they knew what they were talking about. How wonderful it is to learn sympathy through suffering!

Before we close this chapter we must stop and think of

Him who is the greatest sympathizer of all, the Lord Jesus Christ. There is One who can sympathize with us in our sufferings because there is not an experience in our lives about which He does not know. Every valley that we are called upon to pass through, He has passed through ahead of us. He knew what it was to be poor. He knew what it was to be forsaken of friends and left alone. He knew what it was to be thirsty and to be weary. He knew what it was to have enemies revile Him. He knew what it was to spend sleepless nights as He wrestled in prayer for those who did not appreciate Him.

He knew what it was to be tempted and yet to be victorious. He knew what it was to suffer pain as they hung Him upon the cruel cross of Calvary and drove the wicked nails through His precious hands and His precious feet until He cried out, ''My God, my God, why hast thou forsaken me?'' He knew what it meant to go through the valley of the shadow, to taste death for every man. He knew what it was to have the curse of the law with all its blackness and threatening rest upon Him because He bore another's sin. Therefore, today, He is able to help those who are tempted. There is not a thing which is not known to Him.

> For it became him, for whom are all things, and by whom are all things, in bringing many sons unto glory, to make the captain of their salvation perfect through sufferings.
>
> For in that he himself hath suffered being tempted, he is able to help them that are tempted (Hebrews 2:10,18).

O suffering, weary one, look now to the Lord Jesus Christ and receive His comfort!

CHAPTER 7

WHY WE SUFFER

(continued)

IN CONSIDERING the ministry of suffering, we are to remember one primary, basic principle. It is simply this: "whom the Lord loveth he chasteneth." If we belong to Christ, we may expect that He is going to take an interest in our welfare; and since His purpose is to make us like Himself and to bring out in every believer the highest in fruitfulness and service, He expends much labor upon us so that we may become what He desires.

> And we know that all things work together for good to them that love God, to them who are the called according to his purpose.
>   For whom he did foreknow, he also did predestinate to be conformed to the image of his Son, that he might be the firstborn among many brethren (Romans 8:28,29).

I have quoted both verses 28 and 29 because I believe that they are inseparable. God has placed them together. Most Christians are familiar with Romans 8:28. Few indeed would be able to quote the next verse.

However, Romans 8:28 without the next verse is incomplete. Romans 8:28 tells us that all things work together for good to those who love God, but the following verse gives the reason God expends His work and labor upon us. Those whom He did foreknow He predestinated to become like His Son, Jesus Christ. When we realize how unlike Christ most of us are, we begin to recognize the necessity of much work in order to accomplish this purpose.

In another passage of Scripture, God says that He will not withhold any good thing "from them that walk uprightly" before Him. If in the providence of God it is best for us to have trouble and tribulation, we must believe that a loving God will not withhold suffering in order to make us what we ought to be. Remember, the normal path of the believer is one of tribulation. Jesus said, "In this world ye shall have tribulation." And Paul tells us that we must "through much tribulation enter into the kingdom."

So, we may consider this truth as a basic rule: If we do not suffer trouble and tribulation and persecution, it is either because we do not belong to the Lord or because we are worthless from the standpoint of fruit and service. Let us never forget, "whom the Lord loveth he chasteneth."

In past chapters we have seen some of the purposes for which God permits or sends upon us troubles and tribulation — to silence the devil, to glorify God, to make us more like Jesus, to strengthen our faith, to purify our lives, to teach us patience, to make us sympathetic, and to separate us from the world. In this chapter we want to add a few more reasons, although we realize that the list is inexhaustible. The benefits derived from being chastened by the Lord are many and varied. However, there is one we must not fail to mention.

SUFFERING MAKES US AND KEEPS US HUMBLE

God wants His children humble. It was pride that caused the devil to sin; it was pride that caused our first parents to fall. God hates pride. He exalts the humble. And so one of the reasons God places us in the fires of tribulation and testing is that we may learn the most important and indispensable lesson of Christian growth: humility. Probably the best expression of this to be found in Scripture is the example of the apostle Paul. From his writings we notice that he was afflicted with a physical malady which he called a "thorn in the flesh." Many have speculated about the nature of this malady. Some have supposed that Paul was afflicted with ophthalmia as a result of the blinding vision on the day of his conversion. Others believe he was hunchbacked; some say he had a speech impediment; still others suggest that Paul was afflicted with malaria. We are not going to spend time trying to determine which of these is correct. Rather, we are interested in why the Lord permitted this faithful servant of His to suffer throughout the days of his life with this "thorn in the flesh."

In Paul's own account in 2 Corinthians 12 he tells us that at a certain point in his Christian experience he had been caught up into paradise, into the third heaven. There he had received directly from God a revelation which had not been made known to any other. Now, this was a wonderful experience; but Paul, who was the last to claim perfection and who realized that in him, that is, in his flesh, there dwelt no good thing, knew that such an experience might easily be perverted to become the basis of vainglory and fleshly pride. So he tells us,

> And lest I should be exalted above measure through the abundance of the revelations, there was given to me a thorn in the flesh, the messenger of Satan to buffet me, lest I should be exalted above measure.
>
> For this thing I besought the Lord thrice, that it might depart from me.
>
> And he [that is, the Lord] said unto me, My grace is sufficient for thee; for my strength is made perfect in weakness. Most gladly, therefore, will I rather glory in my infirmities, that the power of Christ may rest upon me.
>
> Therefore, I take pleasure in infirmities, in reproaches, in necessities, in persecutions, in distresses for Christ's sake;

for when I am weak, then am I strong (2 Corinthians 12:7-10).

Very little can be added to these words of Paul. He received the definite assurance from the Lord that his "thorn in the flesh"had been given that he might not become proud and puffed up but would remain humble. If he were to lose his humility, God could no longer use him.

Perhaps we can apply this truth to our own hearts and lives. Possibly the reason the Lord does not allow us the relief that we pray for so definitely is this: He knows that to grant the request would only be detrimental to us. As believers we must remember that God always answers prayer, but He does not always answer with a "Yes." Sometimes, in His infinite wisdom, His answer is "No" because He knows what is best for us.

I want to press this point home to those of you who are suffering and have been asking why God does not answer your prayers for healing and restoration. God does answer your prayers. But He probably has not answered them in the way that you wanted. Possibly you have not prayed in His will; you have not made your prayer the prayer of the Savior, "Father, if it be thy will, let this cup pass from me." Our prayers must be in the will of God, for the simple reason that God knows better than we what is good for us.

Let me illustrate. Early in my Christian ministry I was called to apprehend a man who had gone insane. After we had captured him in a field, we found that he carried a loaded revolver. I returned it to his wife, but she said, "I don't want that gun. You'd better keep it, Doctor. I don't want to see it any more." So I took the gun, together with some of the bullets, and brought it to my home. I placed it in one of the drawers of my desk and promptly forgot about it. Then one day my son, Richard, a lad of about five, was rummaging through my study and came upon this revolver and the bullets lying near it. I remember vividly how he came running to me with the revolver in one hand and the bullets in the other hand. Looking up at me, he said, "Daddy, look what I found! May I have this? May I have this?" Now, of course, you who are parents know what I did. He begged me to give him the gun, but quick as a flash I took it away from him, after looking to see whether any bullets had been placed in the magazine. Then I took the bullets away from the boy and said, "No, no, Richard, you cannot have that gun. It's too dangerous for you."

Did my son understand? He did not! He began to cry and plead and beg. There was nothing in all the world he wanted that day more than that beautiful pistol. Nothing else counted. That was the one thing he felt he could not do without. He must have it. But because I was a loving father, and even though he did not understand, I refused his petition. Now that he has grown up, he knows that the best thing for him at that time, even though it caused him pain, was my firm refusal and my answer "No."

Christian friend, are we not like that? We are only children in the faith. We are so limited in our understanding and in our reasoning, but we have a heavenly Father who knows what is best for us. Ofttimes we come to Him and plead and pray and petition for something we think we cannot do without. Yet He says firmly and tenderly, "No, My child, I must refuse this petition. I cannot let you have this thing that you feel you need more than everything else in your life." Although we cannot understand now, I assure you that by-and-by when we meet Him face to face and reach full maturity as children of God, we shall understand.

SUFFERING TEACHES US TO PRAY

I am sure that thousands of you will agree when I tell you that we never learn to pray — really pray — until we are in a place where there is nothing left to do but pray. As long as we can help ourselves, we often neglect the ministry of prayer. But when there is nothing left to do, how effectively we can pray! The greatest people of prayer I have ever known were the greatest sufferers; and the greatest strength in my ministry is the ministry of the thousands who can do little more than pray and write, ''We are praying for you.''

SUFFERING BRINGS REWARDS

There are many results of the ministry of suffering, but one I want to touch on in closing is this: There is a special reward for the suffering. As you know, there are rewards for Christian service, for soul-winning, and for looking for the coming of Christ; but the Lord has set aside a special crown — a special reward — for those who will suffer patiently for Him. Paul tells us,

> If we suffer, we shall also reign with him (2 Timothy 2:12).

There is a special place of service and reigning and power and authority in the kingdom for those who have been the Lord's patient sufferers here below. Peter wrote,

> Beloved, think it not strange concerning the fiery trial which is to test you, as though some strange thing happened unto you,
>
> But rejoice, inasmuch as ye are partakers of Christ's sufferings, that, when his glory shall be revealed, ye may be glad also with exceeding joy (1 Peter 4:12,13).

And in Hebrews 2:10 we are told that Christ was made perfect through suffering.

Someone has aptly said, ''Steel is iron plus fire. Soil is rock plus crushing. Linen is flax plus the comb that separates and the flail that pounds and the shuttle that weaves.'' And the Christian life, if we are to be what God wants us to be, is faith plus suffering. It is God's way of doing things. It is God's own way of making us what we ought to be. God's way is through fire, and through the fire He will perfect us.

CHAPTER 8

WHY ART THOU CAST DOWN?

> Why art thou cast down, O my soul? And why art thou disquieted within me? Hope thou in God; for I shall yet praise him, *who is* the health of my countenance, and my God (Psalm 42:11).

THE "CAST DOWN" believer is an abnormal believer. The happy and rejoicing Christian is the normal Christian. The gloomy Christian is abnormal in that he has not yet learned the proper perspective of life and has not yet learned to interpret and translate all the trials and afflictions of life in terms of future glory and reward. But while the normal Christian is the happy Christian, it is also true that the average Christian is not normal. Sad to say, many believers, while they should be happy, are like David, cast down and complaining bitterly because of their afflictions and trials. Surely there are no people on earth who should be as happy and rejoicing as those who have been redeemed by the precious blood of the Lord Jesus. The Bible says that all things are ours, and someday we shall be heirs of the earth and inherit all things. Let the wealthy have their day now; in the end we shall possess the whole earth. We can afford to wait and be patient, for after a little while He who said He would come will come, and we shall reign with Him over and upon the earth.

ALL THINGS ARE OURS

In the Lord Jesus Christ every believer has a treasure which cannot be described in terms of material wealth and possessions. We are members of the wealthiest and happiest family in all the universe, for God is our Father. He is the Creator of all things. The gold and the silver and the cattle on a thousand hills are His. He is the Father of every believer, and we are heirs of all things that are His. The Son is ours, and we are His. The Lord Jesus Christ gave His life and shed His blood upon Calvary's cross. He broke the bands of death and arose, and today He is seated at the right hand of God the Father in heaven. Soon He is coming again to put down all rule and authority and power and to reign upon this earth in perfect righteousness and justice. And we shall reign with Him. The Holy Spirit is ours — He who came on the day of Pentecost to indwell the body of Christ and every believer. To think that this blessed Holy Spirit, one of the infinite eternal persons of the Trinity, should dwell within our bodies and make them His temples is beyond all comprehension. Salvation is ours; sanctification is ours; glorification is ours. All the promises of the Book are ours. We wait for that glad day when Jesus will come and we shall receive new bodies like the body of our Lord: painless, deathless, sinless bodies in which we shall be able to enjoy to the full all the blessings of the new heaven and the new earth forever and ever. There will be no more weariness, sickness, pain, sorrow, parting, dying, or sinning; but through all eternity, on and on and on and on, forever and ever, we shall enjoy in infinite capacity the "things which God hath prepared for them that love him."

WE SHOULD BE HAPPY

Yes, indeed, when the Christian stops to think what he is by grace and what lies ahead, he should be inexpressibly happy. But sad to say, this is not always true. Too often, like David, we must cry out, "Why art thou cast down, O my soul? And why art thou disquieted within me?" The experience of David is the experience of all of us at some time or another, but we are not alone in these experiences. As we study the saints of the Scriptures, we find that this was the common experience of all. Although we have everything in the world for which to be thankful, it remains a fact that we are still in these frail mortal bodies of ours and are compelled to cope and struggle with the problems of time and material interests.

As we study the Book, we find that even the greatest heroes of the faith had their moments of darkness and despair. They were men of like passions as we are, and when they took their eyes off the Lord and the eternal implications of their present trials, they too cried out, "Why art thou cast down, O my soul?" This was true also of Abraham when he fled the land of Canaan when the Lord sent the famine. Instead of trusting the Lord, he went into Egypt — with tragic results. Moses had his discouraging moments, and Elijah, after his victory over the prophets of Baal, allowed one silly woman, Jezebel, to put him in depression so that he desired to die. Despair came also to the prophets Jonah and Jeremiah, and even John the Baptist had his dark moments. And we could multiply these examples.

DAVID IN THE VALLEY

In this psalm which is the scriptural framework of this message, David, the man of many moods, found himself once more in the valley of gloom and despondency. He cried out, "Why art thou cast down, O my soul. And why art thou disquieted within me?" As he looked out upon the world through his dark glasses, it seemed to David that there was no hope. Hear him as he complains to God:

Lord, how are they increased that trouble me! Many are they that rise up against me.

Many there are who say of my soul, There is no help for him in God. Selah (Psalm 3:1,2).

At times it seems that God is deaf and that the heavens are made of brass, but this is not the usual situation. It is never the fault of God or His promises, but always the fault of the one who complains. In an effort to help those of you who are downcast and discouraged and have had your minds filled with misgivings and doubts, we bring this message. Our text consists of two simple parts: first, a complaint, "Why art thou cast down, O my soul?" and second, the remedy, "Hope thou in God; for I shall yet praise him, who is the health of my countenance, and my God" (Psalm 42:11). Here we have a question and an answer, a diagnosis and a treatment, a complaint and a remedy. As a spiritual physician, we shall first diagnose the disease of soul despondency, and then by His grace administer the remedy of the Word of God.

THE CAUSE OF DESPONDENCY

To arrive at the proper diagnosis of our human despondencies, we must bear in mind certain facts. The first is that we are still in the flesh, and even though we are saved, we still have to contend with bodies that are subject to all sorts of infirmities. Add to this the fact that we also have souls which are subject to varying emotions and highly sensitive to changing circumstances. They are influenced even by the condition of our bodies, as we shall try to point out. Although we are justified in the spirit the moment we believe and receive Christ, our souls need continual sanctification, and our bodies must await complete redemption and glorification at the coming of our Savior. These being facts, we must reckon with them and take them into account. As long as we are here, we must contend with these old bodies of ours, and we cannot escape this struggle.

The Diagnosis

First among the causes of gloom and depression is the natural disposition with which some people come into the world and which they carry with them to their grave. This does not mean that there is no victory over this condition, but merely states a fact that all people, even Christians, are not born with the same cheerful disposition and ability to look on the bright side of life. Some people are born bowed down, and they go to their grave bowed down. They are of a naturally gloomy disposition through no fault of their own. The world would blame them and call them pessimists, but God, who knows all things, takes into consideration their peculiar inherited disposition. Because of hereditary traits and unfortunate circumstances in early life, their natures have been twisted, and they have acquired a cynical attitude toward life.

As a result of the multiplication of these factors, such a person looks at life through dark glasses. Things which may look pink and rosy to another are dismal to him. Do not tell me that when such a person is born again his old nature and natural disposition change. When a man is born again, nothing happens to the old man. Instead, God places within the believer a new man, a new nature, which will never change the old, incorrigible, corrupt nature. It is, however, able to put down and keep in subjection and gain the victory over that old man. But the old remains the old. "That which is born of the flesh is flesh" and always will be flesh. After a man is saved, he still has the old nature and the old disposition to contend with; however, he does not contend in his own strength but in the strength of the new nature and the indwelling Holy Spirit. This is a point that must be constantly borne in mind. Every new man is two men — the old and the new. The old still has all the old characteristics and weaknesses, whereas the new is created in perfect holiness and sinlessness.

SOME EXAMPLES

The Bible abounds with examples of this. The fiery prophet Elijah, even after his tremendous victory over the prophets of Baal, was still subject to his old despondency and wanted to die. The same was true of Jonah and Peter. Peter was the hasty, trigger-finger type, ready to blow off at a moment's notice. After he was saved, he still remained the impetuous Peter and needed the rebuke of Jesus, and even later, the severe public rebuke of Paul. Thomas was a doubter before his conversion, but after he was saved he was still the old Thomas, even though he was a new man. After the Resurrection, he still refused to believe until he had seen the evidences of the nail and spear wounds in the resurrected Jesus.

Am I addressing these words to someone who is included in this category? Perhaps you too are a gloomy Christian. Somehow things always look dark to you, and you cannot help seeing the serious side of every circumstance. I am not endorsing such an attitude. On the contrary, I want to show you how you may have victory over it. Remember first of all that the Lord understands and takes into consideration the fact that you must struggle with a disposition that makes victory doubly difficult; but you can have victory if you will face the issue squarely and remember that God's promises are more dependable than your own feelings.

PHYSICAL INFIRMITIES

A second cause for despondency is physical weakness or illness. Our souls and our bodies are inseparably related, and the feelings of our souls are intimately dependent upon the conditions of our bodies. It is in the spirit that our victory lies, both over the disposition of our souls and the infirmities of our bodies. An aching, suffering body affects our souls, our feelings, and our outlook on life. Frequently people go to the preacher imagining that they have a spiritual problem when the trouble is entirely physical and a doctor could give them more help. In my experience in the practice of medicine, I have seen hundreds of cases where supposedly spiritual problems were actually the result of some physical disease or infirmity. The reverse is also true. Sometimes people imagine that they have physical weaknesses and sicknesses when they are really the result of spiritual disobedience. Many Christians are suffering from weakness and sickness which no doctor can cure because these afflictions are God's chastening upon them for some unconfessed sin.

I do not want to be misunderstood. I do not mean for one moment to intimate that all weaknesses and sicknesses among Christians are the result of unconfessed sin. I am sure that such cases are in the minority. But it is also true that many sicknesses and diseases among believers are the result of God's chastening for unconfessed sin. Paul leaves no doubt in this matter. He wrote the believers at Corinth,

> For this cause many are weak and sickly among you, and many sleep (1 Corinthians 11:30).

The apostle is speaking of believers who refuse to judge sin in their lives and who will not examine themselves, particularly in the light of the teaching concerning the Lord's Supper. Paul says that when the believer knows there is a sin in his life and refuses to put it away by confession and repentance, it may become necessary for the Lord to take a hand in his or her cleansing. He does this by sending sickness and weakness upon that person; and if he persists in his disobedience and unwillingness to repent, He may even take him home by the way of death. God wants us clean and will not tolerate the believer's continuing in known unconfessed sin. He would rather take him home and cleanse him at the judgment seat of Christ.

Therefore, we ought to examine ourselves in the light of His Word and put away all known sin. No Christian can be happy when he knows he is out of the will of the Lord. In the next chapter we shall continue our diagnosis of the disease of Christian despondency and consider some of the mental and spiritual causes of believers being cast down. Then we shall give you the remedy as revealed in the Word of God by the Great Physician Himself.

Are you cast down today? Do you also have to cry out with David, "Why art thou cast down, O my soul? And why art thou disquieted within me?" Then do this: examine your own heart and see if the trouble lies in your own life. Is there a spirit of disobedience and rebellion? Is there sin in your life? Take God's remedy: "If we confess our sins, he is faithful and just to forgive us our sins, and to cleanse us from all unrighteousness." Then claim the promises of God and remember that your salvation depends upon *His* word — not *your* feelings.

CHAPTER 9

WHY ART THOU CAST DOWN?

(continued)

DAVID WAS IN the deep valley of despair when he wrote the 42nd Psalm. As he looked about him and saw the wicked prospering and the righteous suffering, he was at a loss to know the meaning of it all, and his heart was despondent. He spent his time weeping and lamenting, as we read in verse 3,

> My tears have been my food day and night, while they continually say unto me, Where is thy God? (Psalm 42:3).

He could not understand God's mysterious dealings. He had searched his heart; he remembered how he had served the Lord. Yet he found himself in the deepest distress. To David it seemed that the Lord was fast asleep and utterly oblivious and indifferent to his sad state and his deep depression. In Psalm 44 he cried,

> Awake, why sleepest thou, O Lord? Arise, cast us not off forever.
> Wherefore hidest thou thy face, and forgettest our affliction and our oppression?
> For our soul is bowed down to the dust; our belly cleaveth unto the earth.
> Arise for our help, and redeem us for thy mercies' sake (Psalm 44:23-26).

David was surely in a bad way. Everything seemed dark. His prayers apparently were unanswered, and it seemed as if his great God had fallen asleep and was deliberately hiding His face from him. What evil thoughts Satan places in our minds when we get our eyes on our troubles and off the Lord and His wise providence! Then, to make matters worse, the enemy began to taunt him and said, "Where is thy God? Where is the God in whom you boasted and rejoiced? Where is He whom you praised so loudly a few days ago? Now here you sit, a child of the God whom you worship, and you moan and groan and cry and weep and complain and are in despair." He was about to abandon all hope; then he achieved the proper perspective. He realized what caused his depression and turned to God as the only cure for his trouble and difficulty.

MANY CAUSES OF DEPRESSION

In the previous chapter we tried to point out a few reasons for the depression of spirit which Christians often experience. We are not merely spirit even after we are saved. We still have souls and bodies. The body is heir to all sorts of human weakness and pain and suffering, while the soul is subject to varying and changing emotions and feelings, and these often affect our spiritual outlook. We must, as we have said, recognize the fact that until we receive our redeemed bodies, we must cope with the weakness of the flesh and the temptations of the soul.

We pointed out that many of God's children are depressed and cast down because of their naturally gloomy dispositions. Some have happy, carefree dispositions; others are always conscious of life's serious side. In order to have victory, these dispositions must be made subject to the new nature. There are also physical weaknesses which tremendously affect our spiritual outlook and our joy of soul. It is a great deal easier to be happy and to praise God when all is bright and prosperous. This is true of the businessman — the Christian businessman. When business is good and things are going fine, it is easy to praise the Lord. I hear some pious soul say, "We should always be happy, even when things are bad." I quite agree that we should, but the fact remains that it is much easier to praise the Lord when we are healthy than when we are racked with pain and burning with fever.

Many times people have come to me with spiritual complaints and deep depression of spirits caused by some physical malady or sickness. They needed the advice of a doctor more than the counsel of a preacher. I remember one case in particular. A dear saint of God found herself in the deepest valley of despair because she imagined she had committed the sin against the Holy Spirit. She was driven almost to insanity. She traveled from preacher to preacher seeking relief, but the darkness only deepened. When she came to me, I was led to suggest that she go to a physician instead and find out if there was not some physical cause for her mental depression. Upon examination it was found that she was gradually being poisoned by badly infected teeth. A dentist removed the cause. In three weeks her depression was gone, and she was again the happy Christian she had been formerly. I do not recommend tooth extraction for all cases of mental and spiritual depression, but I merely want to emphasize the fact that the condition of our bodies affects our souls and our outlook on life. It is foolish to ignore this.

YELLOW WINDOWS AND A YELLOW WORLD

It is a known fact that certain diseases affect people differently. Some diseases are accompanied by an optimistic outlook, whereas others tend to cause pessimism. We know that tuberculosis, especially pulmonary tuberculosis, is usually characterized by cheerfulness of disposition, whereas such diseases as diabetes and stomach and liver trouble are predisposing causes of grouchiness and depression. I am not finding fault, but as a physician I am urging you to face certain facts in order that I may the better help you to overcome these natural predispositions. If your soul is cast down because of a sluggish liver, it might be well to take, with your prayers, a few doses of calomel. If your whole body is jaundiced, you cannot help looking out of the windows of your soul upon a greenish-yellow world.

One man who suffered from a spiritual depression so deep that he wanted to die was thoroughly cured by a good meal. This man, you may recall, was Elijah. He surely was dejected. He ran for his life and became very tired and faint. He lay down under a juniper tree and asked the Lord to let him die. But the Lord said, "Elijah, all you need is a good meal and a long nap and you will be all right." God prepared a good meal; Elijah had a good sleep, and he got up and went in the strength of it forty days. He went into the wilderness and lived to be a mighty prophet who served the Lord for many years. The man who wanted to die never died, for he was translated into heaven.

MENTAL DISEASES

What is true of physical weakness is true also of mental illness. There is no question that many of the maladies of spirit from which God's dear children suffer are in their heads, not their hearts. Certain mental diseases are accompanied by depression and despair. Notwithstanding, it is true that many times our troubles are truly of a spiritual nature. Much of this distress is due to ignorance concerning God's plan for our lives, ignorance of the promises of God, failure to confess our sins, and selfishness in our prayers. First, let me again emphasize unconfessed sin as the prime cause of much doubt and spiritual depression. If there is sin in the Christian's life, there cannot be joy and victory. Perhaps that sin is nothing more than failure to believe and appropriate the promises of God.

A distorted conception of the love of God may cause spiritual gloom and despair. Some people have sat all their lives under the twisted preaching about a God who is anything but a God of love and compassion. There are thousands of people whose lives are one sad dirge of gloom and doubt because they have been taught that the plan of salvation is more difficult than it is. They think they must *do* something to be saved — live perfect lives, keep the law, work, toil, and worry. One day, when they have lived in comparative victory, they are happy. The next, when they have failed, they moan and cry that they are lost again. They dwell only upon those isolated texts in Scripture which have no application to their lives at all. Two things must be kept in mind. First, salvation is all of grace and does not depend in the least upon our goodness, works, religion, success, or keeping the law. Second, God has also made a provision that when saved people fail, they can receive cleansing and forgiveness through simple confession:

> If we confess our sins, he is faithful and just to forgive us our sins, and to cleanse us from all unrighteousness (1 John 1:9).

BEREAVEMENT AND SORROW

Another common cause of gloom is bereavement and sorrow. Let me repeat that it is much easier to rejoice in the Lord when your family is well than when you sit beside the sickbed or even the casket of one who was dearer than life to you. That is the time the devil taunts you and points to others who live in sin and wickedness and never seem to have any trials or troubles. And he says, "You! Are you a child of God? If there is a God in heaven, why does He permit these things?" David also had that experience. Hear him in Psalm 73:

> But as for me, my feet were almost gone; my steps had almost slipped.

For I was envious at the foolish, when I saw the prosperity of the wicked.

For there are no pangs in their death; but their strength is firm.

Their eyes stand out with fatness; they have more than heart could wish.

And they say, How doth God know? And is there knowledge in the Most High?

Behold, these are the ungodly, who prosper in the world; they increase in riches.

Verily, I have cleansed my heart in vain, and washed my hands in innocence.

For all the day long have I been plagued, and chastened every morning (Psalm 73:2,3,4,7,11-14).

Here, indeed, was a problem, and when David considered how the wicked prospered and the righteous suffered, he cried out in despair,

When I thought to know this, it was too painful for me (Psalm 73:16).

But now notice the next word in verse 17:

Until I went into the sanctuary of God; then understood I their end.

Surely, thou didst set them in slippery places; thou castedst them down into destruction.

For, lo, they that are far from thee shall perish; thou hast destroyed all those who play the harlot departing from thee.

But it is good for me to draw near to God; I have put my trust in the Lord God, that I may declare all thy works (Psalm 73:17,18,27,28).

Note well that word "until." David looked beyond the present and saw two things. First, he saw that the wicked were doomed to punishment and that God was dealing with His own child in love, preparing him for a glory which could come only through suffering and pain. When we interpret our troubles in terms of the future and eternity, then all is bright. How much better to suffer for a little while as a child of God than to be cast into an eternal hell forever as a sinner! God does not chasten those who are not His. He lets them go. There is only judgment and hell for them at the end of the road. But He is constantly working to make you who are His ready for the glory. Remember, Paul said,

> For our light affliction, which is but for a moment, worketh for us a far more exceeding and eternal weight of glory,
>   While we look not at the things which are seen, but at the things which are not seen; for the things which are seen are temporal, but the things which are not seen are eternal (2 Corinthians 4:17,18).

Yes, God is working out a pattern in our lives. We see only the present and the immediate, but God sees the whole picture of one's life as it will appear when the last stroke of the brush has completed the picture. In this pattern of our lives there are bright spots and dark backgrounds, all of them necessary for the complete portrait. As we pass through the dark experiences of life, we see only that dark piece. Our experiences resemble a jigsaw puzzle. Here is a black piece which seems to fit nowhere at all. It does not make sense. Here is a little brighter piece. Other sections of the jigsaw puzzle are dark, and some pitch black, and we cry and moan in these black moments. But by-and-by the Master will take all the pieces which look so disconnected to us now and will carefully arrange each piece in its proper place. Then we shall see His completed work — the work of a Master who makes no mistakes. Listen, when it is all ready, we shall find that the dark pieces of the puzzle were as important to the completion of the full beauty of the pattern as the bright sections.

Take heart, dear child of God. Father makes no mistakes. He loves you more than you love Him, and even as the child cannot understand the rod of an earthly father until he reaches

maturity, so, too, we cannot understand all now. But someday we shall understand.

> Now we see through a glass darkly, but then we shall see his
> face clearly. Now we see only the separate parts and pieces,
> but then we shall know it in its perfectness, even as he knows
> now (1 Corinthians 13:12, free translation).

CHAPTER 10

WHY ART THOU CAST DOWN?

(continued)

"IN THE WORLD ye shall have tribulation: but be of good cheer; I have overcome the world," said Jesus to His disciples. Until the Christian faces this fact, he will never be able to have the victory of faith which overcomes the world. Just as surely as God saves you, He also begins a good work in you which will never cease until He has accomplished His purpose of making you like His Son, Jesus Christ.

Our Father does not always explain why He allows us to pass through many dark experiences. He wants us to develop and exercise our faith, without which it is impossible to please God. David's complaint in Psalm 42 was a bitter one. When he looked upon the wicked and saw how they prospered and how God's people seemed always to be tested and tried, he came to the point of despair. But when he sat down soberly with the Word of God and came to that place of complete submission to God's will, he could rejoice even in tribulation. And that is the victory, which is the only cure for spiritual depression and gloom.

We have tried in the previous chapters to point out that our feelings are very much dependent upon many things. Our circumstances, our environment, our natural disposition, our physical and mental health, and the struggle we have with the flesh all have a bearing upon our feelings and our outlook upon life. They often cause us to cry out, "Why art thou cast down, O my soul?" But thanks be to God, the Great Physician is equal to them all. He has the remedy and He never fails. So after having tried to diagnose the case, we shall attempt in this chapter to show you the cure.

In David's psalms, there are five well-defined steps. If followed, they will bring the same joy and victory David experienced and then recorded for all the generations of suffering and despairing ones in all ages.

1. REMEMBER some things you have forgotten. David first remembered the wrong thing. In Psalm 42:4 he said, "When I remember these things, I pour out my soul in me."

But he was remembering his troubles, his tears and suffering, and the taunts of the wicked. And the more he thought on his own trouble, the worse he felt. But after his third cry of "Why art thou cast down?" in Psalm 43:5, there was a change in David:

> We have heard with our ears, O God; our fathers have told us what work thou didst in their days, in times of old.
>
> How thou didst drive out the nations with thy hand, and plantedst them; how thou didst afflict the people, and cast them out.
>
> For they got not the land in possession by their own sword, neither did their own arm save them, but thy right hand, and thine arm, and the light of thy countenance, because thou hadst a favor unto them (Psalm 44:1-3).

Yes, he remembered that God had never failed his fathers in days of old. Many were their dark days and experiences, but in the end God was always faithful. The psalmist must have remembered what he had written in the 34th Psalm, when he was on the mountaintop and not in the valley of despair. In this psalm, David had written,

Many are the afflictions of the righteous; but the Lord delivereth him out of them all (Psalm 34:19).

This, my friend, is the first thing you must do. Stop and think back. Has God ever failed? Oh, yes, the days have been dark, but in the end has He ever failed? I know what your answer is. Well, then, He will not fail you now. In the end you will see the glory of the Lord through your deepest afflictions. Remember, and when you do, you will be ashamed that you ever doubted Him at all.

2. READ THE WORD. Go to the Scriptures. David could only remember what God had done in the past by turning to the record of the Word of the Lord. And as he read that record of God's faithfulness, his soul was restored. May I suggest that much of the gloom and the despair of Christians in every age is because they have been too occupied with their troubles and have neglected the precious promises of the Word. Among the thousands of victorious sufferers I have been privileged to know in my ministry, I have found that a knowledge of the Word and victory in trial and suffering are inseparably associated. I have seen patient sufferers who had lain in pain upon beds of illness for years and yet radiated joy and happiness and perfect peace because they appropriated the precious promises of God. I do not doubt for one moment that the Lord sometimes places us upon our backs in order that we may have more time to study His Word. Many of us are too busy when we are well to give proper attention to the study of His Word, and then the Lord lays us aside so that we will have time for this most important and indispensable need in our Christian lives.

3. PRAY. No Christian can grow without much prayer. I say *much* prayer. The habitual, perfunctory prayers we offer on set occasions, in the morning, at evening, and at mealtime,

are commendable, but if they are the extent of our prayer life, we will be spiritually impoverished. Many Christians have been laid aside for just one reason: that God might teach them the importance of prayer. Many of us, and that includes myself, never really learned to cry out to God in deep earnestness until we were put in a corner where we could do nothing else. And God's sufferers have always been the best pray-ers. All over the world the Lord has thousands of saints whom He has laid aside in their homes and upon their beds because they are effective pray-ers. Sometimes we wonder why God does not raise up these precious saints who lay upon beds year after year. Do you know why? It would mean an irreparable loss to the entire church of Jesus Christ. I could not preach were it not for that great army of prayer warriors, many of whom God permits to remain behind with the stuff in order that they may pray. If they were well, their time for prayer might be limited because of the many other duties, but their prayers are needed — yea, they are indispensable — and so while others carry the burden in the public, active service, the faithful laid-aside ones carry the burden in the private but equally active chamber of prayer.

4. HAVE FAITH AND HOPE. Notice how the complaint of David ends. He says,

> Hope in God; for I shall yet praise him, who is the health of my countenance, and my God (Psalm 43:5).

He declares, in effect, "Hope thou in God, for I shall yet praise Him. This trouble may be severe, but it is only for a moment. It will not last, and someday the sun is going to break through again." I like the homely philosophy of the preacher who said, "My favorite text in the Bible is: 'It came to pass.' I like that text, and it gives me so much comfort. 'It came to pass.' Yes, all my troubles come to pass. They won't last. When I am sick I say, 'It came to pass.' When I am in trouble, 'It came to pass.' '' That may be a simple philosophy, but it is effective. In our lives, too, these things come to pass; but more than that, they are for a definite purpose. God does not permit even one thing to happen to us without a divine and wise purpose, which we shall know by-and-by.

The hope of the future is the cure for every ill of the Christian. It is not for us to unravel the mystery now; it is enough to know that He doeth all things well and that ''all things work together for good to them that love God.''

To the world it may seem that it does not pay to serve the Lord. And even to us the way may often be dark, and we cannot see how these present experiences can be of value. But we are to judge all things in the light of His coming and the giving of rewards. Paul says,

> Therefore, judge nothing before the time, until the Lord come, who both will bring to light the hidden things of darkness, and will make manifest the counsels of the hearts; and then shall every man have praise of God (1 Corinthians 4:5).

This is a very precious truth. There is a time of reckoning coming, and then we shall all receive from His hand the rewards based upon all the circumstances of life. Man judges by the outward appearance, but God will judge not only our deeds but our motives and our opportunities as well. He will take into consideration the struggles we have had, not the apparent victory. God knows that it is easier for some people to live a joyous, victorious life than for others. And He will take that knowledge into account. He knows that it is easier to live a happy life when all goes well than when one is afflicted as so many are. The Lord will take this into account and give a special reward to those who have apparently done the least because of the limitations of life.

Many a humble saint of God who suffered upon the bed of

affliction will receive a greater reward than some flaming preacher who stirred thousands and saw countless numbers coming to Christ under his ministry. That dear soul upon that bed, whose name never made the papers, did what she could in patient suffering and prayer with the limited opportunities and talents she had, while the preacher wasted his spiritual substance in luxury and ease. Yes, God will judge on the basis of opportunity and faithfulness, and there will be many surprises in heaven. When the rewards are given out, I expect to take a seat far behind some of you precious souls whose voices are never heard by the public.

At that day and at that reckoning, God will take into account all things. He will remember that it is easier for some to live a victorious life than for others. It is easier to live for Jesus when all is prosperous than when all is sorrow and pain. One who has a faithful wife who stands by and helps finds it easier to live for Christ than one who is married to an unbeliever. It is easier for some wives to be cheerful and happy who have godly, understanding husbands than for others who have unfaithful, drunken husbands. The Lord will take that into account, too. It is easier for working people who have Christian employers to live for Christ than for some who work for employers who curse and swear and blaspheme. It is easier if you work in a Christian office or institution than if you must work in a factory or establishment where smut and vileness and cursing are heard continually. We may criticize some who seem to have a struggle, but if we could see as God sees and know how much more trying their environment is, we would not judge.

Even our dispositions will be taken into account. Some people are even-tempered. It is no effort for them to control themselves. They are "born that way" and retain that control. Others come into the world with the fiery disposition of a Peter. After they are saved, they still have that same old flesh and disposition, and while they should have victory, no one but God knows the hard battle they wage, a battle which those of you who do not have the same temper or disposition know nothing about. Many people who seem to live the victorious life do not fight a battle nearly so difficult as that waged by others who are apparently defeated. I thank God that when the rewards are handed out, the Judge is going to take all this into account.

Yes, beloved, soon the Lord will come, and then we shall understand. That is what David meant when he cried out, "Hope thou in God; for I shall yet praise him." And that is the final step.

5. PRAISE HIM AT ALL TIMES. We have a bright tomorrow. Soon the day of His coming will be here, and then we shall know as we are known:

> For now we see in a mirror, darkly; but then, face to face; now I know in part, but then shall I know even as also I am known (1 Corinthians 13:12).

CHAPTER 11

HIS GRACE IS SUFFICIENT

For our light affliction, which is but for a moment, worketh for us a far more exceeding and eternal weight of glory,

While we look not at the things which are seen, but at the things which are not seen; for the things which are seen are temporal, but the things which are not seen are eternal (2 Corinthians 4:17,18).

WHY ARE SO many Christians afflicted? Why do God's people suffer? These are questions which are asked a thousand times a day by multitudes of God's dear people afflicted and smitten, suffering and languishing, bowed down with grievous burdens and heavy loads. The Bible has the answer. Suffering is not an abnormal experience among believers. Rather, the Christian who does not suffer, who does not have a thorn in the flesh, is abnormal. Jesus said, "In the world ye shall have tribulation," and in Acts we read that we "must through much tribulation enter into the kingdom of God." So let us accept the truth that being a Christian does not exempt us from affliction and suffering. To be a child of God subjects us to additional suffering, for God does not chasten the devil's children, but disciplines those who are His very own. "Whom the Lord loveth he chasteneth." If you are being chastened today, you should be thankful the Lord has set His love upon you enough to chasten you and that He does not let you drift without His restraining and disciplining hand.

HIS GRACE IS SUFFICIENT

The Lord not only permits His children to suffer affliction and pass under the rod, but He also provides the needed grace to bear whatever He may send upon them. When Paul prayed three times to have his thorn in the flesh removed, the Lord answered, "My grace is sufficient for thee" (2 Corinthians 12:9). But even beyond that, the Lord has revealed that everything He sends the believer is for His own glory and for the believer's good. Everything that happens to us has some bearing on our future glory and the joys of heaven and eternity.

In 2 Corinthians 4:17,18, Paul gives us a glimpse into the purposes of God in sending afflictions upon us. Notice the words, "our light affliction." This is a remarkable statement from the pen of Paul. When we consider what he endured during the years after his conversion, we wonder how the apostle could say, "our light affliction." From the day he was converted, he had been afflicted. He had been imprisoned, shipwrecked, beaten, scourged, maligned, threatened, and stoned. He had known poverty, want, and hunger; and besides the ignominy of being rejected by his own nation and hounded from place to place, he was afflicted with a thorn in the flesh, a messenger of Satan to buffet him. Before his life was over, he would be falsely accused, imprisoned, condemned, and finally beheaded for the cause of Christ whom he loved. "Is this a light affliction?" we ask. "Yes," says Paul, "it is a light affliction."

None of us has suffered as Paul did, and yet how often we murmur and repine and become discouraged and blue and downhearted and feel that our lot is worse than that of anyone else on earth! It is well, therefore, for us to give heed to the words of a man who suffered more than anyone else, and all of it for the sake of his love for the Lord Jesus Christ. "Yes," says Paul, "it is but a light affliction."

It Is But for a Moment

Paul makes his statement all the more striking when he tells us that the affliction is only for a little while. He says, "Our light affliction, which is but for a moment."

As far as we can determine, Paul served the Lord Jesus for more than thirty-five years from the day he met the Lord on the way to Damascus; and he calls those thirty-five years of suffering and affliction, of privation and starvation, of beatings and imprisonments, only a "moment." What right have we, as believers, who have not been so faithful to or zealous for our Lord as Paul was, to expect that we shall escape these things which Paul experienced? And yet all too often we think that the pathway of the Christian should be roses and sunshine and that when we have troubles and tribulations there is something wrong. It was not thus with Paul, or Job, or David, or Isaiah, or Jeremiah, or John the Baptist, or James, or Peter, or John, or Paul. If the Lord does not send us affliction and trials, we may well doubt whether the Lord sees in us anything worthy of development. The more fruitful your life, the more the Lord will cultivate it, and plow it, and bestow labor upon it. No plow point ever pierces the barren desert sands; but the more productive the field, the more it is plowed. So, too, with the Lord. Our worth to Christ may often be measured by the trials and the testings which He sends upon us. Undoubtedly it was because Paul realized this that he could call his grievous troubles a "light affliction . . . for a moment."

Only Fire Purifies

God's purpose in saving men and women is to make them ultimately like their Savior, the Lord Jesus Christ. John says:

Beloved, now are we the children of God, and it doth not yet appear what we shall be; but we know that, when he shall appear, we shall be like him; for we shall see him as he is (1 John 3:2).

God's purpose in choosing us was to make us like His Son Jesus. In Romans 8 we read,

For whom he did foreknow, he also did predestinate to be conformed to the image of his Son, that he might be the firstborn among many brethren (Romans 8:29).

That process of making us like Jesus begins here and now. God is not going to let us be as unlike His Son as possible and then suddenly when He comes, change us into His likeness. The Lord is busy even now seeking to make us more Christ-like. And that cannot be done without suffering. The Holy Spirit tells us that even Jesus was not made perfect without suffering. Testing, trial, suffering, and chastening are God's way of purifying and cleansing and conforming His children to the image of His Son.

Suffering one, upon your bed of illness, do you realize why you are here? God is making you like His Son, and in His wise providence this is one of the ways He is accomplishing it.

NOT NOW, BUT THEN

The greatest comfort which God has given to His afflicted ones is the assurance that all our suffering here below will be fully and completely and superabundantly rewarded by-and-by with a glory so great and unspeakable that the trials of this life will truly seem like light afflictions which were indeed only for a moment. The sufferer's crown is one of the most precious crowns which God will give His children. He associates suffering with a special crown of glory. James tells us,

Blessed is the man that endureth temptation; for when he is tried, he shall receive the crown of life, which the Lord hath promised to them that love him (James 1:12).

Peter also speaks of this,

Beloved, think it not strange concerning the fiery trial which is to test you, as though some strange thing happened unto you,

But rejoice, inasmuch as ye are partakers of Christ's sufferings, that, when his glory shall be revealed, ye may be glad also with exceeding joy (1 Peter 4:12,13).

Paul assures Timothy that "if we suffer, we shall also reign with him." Oh, there is a glory for those who suffer patiently here below!

WHILE WE LOOK NOT

Paul says in our theme text,

For our light affliction, which is but for a moment, worketh for us a far more exceeding and eternal weight of glory,

While we look not at the things which are seen, but at the things which are not seen; for the things which are seen are temporal, but the things which are not seen are eternal (2 Corinthians 4:17,18).

Notice verse 18 carefully. Paul says that our afflictions seem light and brief if we look at them in the right way. While we look at them in a temporal way, only in light of the present, they are heavy and wearisome. But if we look beyond the temporal to the future, to the time of rewards, our sufferings are nothing by comparison. Do you get the point Paul is trying to make? He says, "Interpret your trials in the light of eternity and the future glory." As we suffer, we think of what God is doing and the glory He is preparing and the rewards we shall receive for patient endurance when Jesus comes. A few years of suffering is short compared with eternity. These burdens are light in comparison with the weight of glory that shall be revealed in us. The price we pay now is nothing compared with the wealth which is awaiting us. Look at your troubles alone, and you go down. Look at the glory ahead and realize what God in love is preparing you for, and you can still praise Him through your tears.

Jesus Our Example

Jesus viewed all things in the light of eternity. The writer of Hebrews tells us,

> Wherefore, seeing we also are compassed about with so great a cloud of witnesses, let us lay aside every weight, and the sin which doth so easily beset us, and let us run with patience the race that is set before us,
>
> Looking unto Jesus, the author and finisher of our faith, who for the joy that was set before him endured the cross, despising the shame, and is set down at the right hand of the throne of God (Hebrews 12:1,2).

Jesus suffered beating, spitting, pain, reviling, scoffing, suffering, agony, and death on the cross for the joy that was set before Him — the joy of saving others — the joy of bringing many sons to glory. As a mother bears the pain and the agony for the joy of hearing her child's cry, so Jesus suffered joyfully. It is all in the way we look at our trials. Interpreted in terms of coming glory and eternity, they are light and "but for a moment."

Are you afflicted and suffering, precious child of God? Then remember — your Father still knows best, and He has something wonderful for you. Grapes must be crushed before wine can be made. Unless the violin string is stretched until it cries out in pain, there is no music in it. Wheat must be broken to make bread. We may not know what God is doing now, but someday we shall understand and be like Him.

An anonymous poet has written these words of comfort:

> If we could push ajar the gates of life,
> And stand within and all God's workings see,

We could interpret all this doubt and strife,
    And for each mystery we'd find the key.

But not today! Then be content, poor heart;
    God's plans like lilies pure and white unfold;
We must not tear the close-shut leaves apart:
    Time will reveal the calyxes of gold.

And when through patient toil we reach the land
    Where tired feet with sandals loosed may rest,
When we shall clearly know and understand,
    I know that we shall say God's way was best.

DATE DUE

DEC 4 1988			
OCT 0 9 '99			
GAYLORD			PRINTED IN U.S.A